"Most of us are familiar with the power of the messages about how to live our lives received early in life, when we were too young to know better. Many of us believe that these early messages were the best we could get considering all of the human factors. However, many of these messages had the effect of crippling our present lives. The inevitable question comes up—Is there anything we can do to change these messages and get better guides for ourselves? Mr. Hoffman's book has a great deal to offer in relation to this question. He comes to this change through using his psychic knowledge to develop creative ways to come to more useful guidance for our lives. In the usual sense, his approach is unconventional and for many would be considered far out. In this day and age when the unconventional of today becomes the normal of tomorrow, Mr. Hoffman's book might well point in the direction of the normal."

Virginia Satir
International teacher of Family Therapy
Author of *Peoplemaking* and *Conjoint Family Therapy*

"Every Pastor in America, regardless of their denomination, affiliation, or theology, should read this book."

Reverend George McLaird, Pastor
Sausalito Presbyterian Church

"The Quadrinity Process is the best method I know for the re-alignment of relationships with parents and parent surrogates and, more generally, a powerful tool in the service of the development of love for self and others."

Claudio Naranjo, M.D.
Author of *The One Quest*

"It is a thorough and exhaustive procedure which can save people a lot of time in growing . . . those who have been disappointed in other searches can find what they are looking for here."

Lee Sannella, M.D.
Author of *Kundalini: Psychosis or Transcendence?*

"It will replace psychoanalysis."

Jerry Rubin
Author of *Growing Up at 37*

"We have the capacity to become the person we want to be. Yet we often face a major obstacle—the emotional patterns we learned in childhood. Here, a noted therapist vividly explains how to unravel the confining web of one's childhood experiences, and move boldly beyond them."

Cosmopolitan

"Bob Hoffman's book may prove to be one of the most important publications of any recent year . . . The fundamental message—that to love others we must first love and know ourselves—goes back, of course, to Erich Fromm, to Socrates, to the world's major religions. The Quadrinity Process, however, does not command us to love, but removes the barriers that prevent us from loving . . . The author writes clearly and forcefully. No one has ever accused Bob Hoffman of pulling his punches—yet his deep compassion shines through."

William Carter
San Francisco Bay Guardian

"I urge you to beg, borrow, buy, or even steal a copy. Your reward will be enormous."

Leo F. King
Librarian, *San Francisco Book Club*

"I have a strong feeling of contentment with my life, and appreciation of the Quadrinity Process for its role in helping me make some necessary changes . . . The Quadrinity Process was a catalyst that speeded up, clarified and perhaps, simplified the process of change."

Elizabeth Fishel
Human Behavior

"Hoffman seems to have the power to assist ordinary neurotics help heal themselves."

Kevin Starr
San Francisco Examiner

NO ONE IS TO BLAME

Freedom From Compulsive Self-Defeating Behavior

NO ONE IS TO BLAME

Freedom From Compulsive Self-Defeating Behavior

The Discoveries of the Quadrinity Process

by Bob Hoffman

RECYCLING BOOKS
Oakland, California

Formerly published by Science and Behavior Books, Inc. under the same title. Previously published by E. P. Dutton & Co., Inc. under the title: *Getting Divorced from Mother & Dad: The Discoveries of the Fischer-Hoffman Process.*

RECYCLING BOOKS
2861 Chelsea Drive, Oakland, CA 94611

International Standard Book Number: 0-8314-0057-9
Library of Congress Catalog Card Number: 79-63271

*I lovingly dedicate this book
to the living spirit of Dr. Siegfried Fischer,
scientist, neurologist, and psychiatrist
of great wisdom and deep compassion for mankind.*

In the interest of confidentiality the names of the case histories reported herein have been changed. Any resemblance to others living or dead is purely coincidental.

TABLE OF CONTENTS

FOREWORD

Some years ago Donovan Bess, then a *San Francisco Chronicle* reporter, introduced me to Bob Hoffman. At that time Bob was offering his services in an eight-session process in which he employed himself as a psychic, assisting his clients toward an expansion of love.

When I came upon him I had been through many therapies and "worked things out," so I did not expect a dramatic experience. Yet at the end I had to agree with Bob that never before had I formed such a coherent picture of the action of parental influences in my development. As I look back after four years, I continue to regard it as a significant impact in my life.

It seems to me, going through this process, that even though Bob was a gifted healer of souls, the success of his work did not rest upon this personal ingredient alone. His therapeutic guided trip—a well-organized package of procedures comprising the analysis of early experiences, abreactions, and extensive use of imagery—seemed to me a technical conception that could be further developed and effectively used by others, without his psychic ability.

Within a short time I was employing a group adaptation of the process (which I called the "Fischer-Hoffman Process") in a group for psychological and spiritual development that I led at the time—the beginnings of Seekers After Truth (SAT). The results seemed good enough to invite further exploration, and months later my collaborators, Rosalyn Shaffer and Kathleen Speeth, were employing the method in two other SAT groups. Bob attended Rosalyn's group as an observer, and though he disapproved in many regards, he appreciated the workability of the group application. Bob then generated the alternative form. His way was better in his hands than our attempt had been, and proof of my conviction is that some two hundred people in SAT groups have experienced Bob's approach as part of their program, either under his direction or that of his apprentices.

The Fischer-Hoffman wave has reached Chile and Spain, Israel and India and I am happy to believe that I have incurred some good karma by playing John the Baptist in this story.

Months ago, I was invited by Michael Toms, director of New Dimensions, to participate in a public meeting and broadcast in San Francisco with Bob and several psychologists. Addressing myself in answer to a question as to what I regarded as characteristic of the Fischer-Hoffman Process, I made the following statement:

> *There has been a tendency in psychotherapy ever since the dawn of psychoanalysis to emphasize the therapeutic aspects of unstructured situations. To begin with, psychoanalysis was built around the technique of free association, a situation in which a person says whatever comes to mind. Whatever the value of interpretation, there is value in free association (which is a relinquishing of structure) because in the ordinary social situation, we are, in one way or another, playing a game with implicit rules.*
>
> *The therapeutic aspects of unstructuring have culminated in encounter groups and similar situations where a group of people meet without rules in an open situation that summons the creative aspects of the person.*
>
> *As distinct from this most predominant therapeutic tendency, the Fischer-Hoffman Process is highly structured. I believe that this is a time in which there are so many strategies which are known in psychotherapy that it is possible to package a process where these are systematically included.*
>
> *Another aspect of the Process, as I see it, is its being in many ways counter counter-culture. The counter-culture has emphasized the here-and-now*

and disdained the past, for instance, and the Fischer-Hoffman approach takes us back to the past, just as psychoanalysis did at the beginning. Freud's original insight was that people who suffered from neurosis are suffering from memories. So the intent of therapy was to elucidate these memories and their associations. The chief concept of psychoanalysis is, perhaps, that of transference. Our relationships with people are not only seen as transference in the sense that they are the reenactment of the parental relationships, but in that they fall short of the fullness of life. We are not living if we are acting as automatons according to programming. So the early psychoanalytic attempt was to understand transference by analyzing the parental situation.

Yet in recent years, psychotherapy has moved more and more into understanding and repairing the present. Gestalt therapy, which is the approach that I have practiced most, was, I think, the most significant voice in bringing about a cultural understanding of this. The here-and-now came to stand in opposition to the endless elucidation of the past. And yet, Fritz Perls, the creator of Gestalt therapy, had many, if not most, of his greatest successes, I believe, when he would follow the thread from present to past and work on what was happening with one or the other of the parents. So that even though Gestalt embraced the here-and-now ideologically, in practice it absorbed much of psychoanalysis. If the creed of Gestalt therapy were to be taken literally, this approach would miss the working out of the past. I believe, like Bob, that our capacity to love others is rooted in our ability to love ourselves, and that this goes hand in hand with the state of our relationships with our parents.

I know Bob to be a good storyteller, and hope that his gift as a communicator brings some of his healing influence to you.

Claudio Naranjo

ACKNOWLEDGEMENTS

With love and deepest gratitude I thank all my students whose participation has helped the Quadrinity Process to develop and grow, and Dr. Claudio Naranjo who has facilitated the introduction of our work throughout the world.

I want to express my love and heartfelt gratitude to Dennis Briskin who worked so closely with me in bringing this work to its present form. This book would not be what it is without his skillful and imaginative writing assistance.

CHAPTER I

HOW'S YOUR LOVE LIFE?

Asking about your love life is a rude way to begin a book. On the other hand, it quickly gets to what matters: how you are living your life right now.

This book is filled with rude, provocative questions to help you take an honest look at yourself. While looking honestly may be difficult and sometimes painful, the reward is worth it because seeing it as it really is is the first step toward resolution.

Fear of the pain blinds us to the goal of healing. Only by seeing our problems clearly and experiencing them can we do something about them. There really is a way to arrive at something better than life as we may have known it, no matter how completely we may have given in to despair— even if only periodically. There is a way out. Others have done it and gone on to live lives of fulfillment and peace, with no inner conflicts or anxieties. So can you.

The way out begins by answering the question: How *is* your love life? Do you have warm, loving people in your life? People who know you well and love you? People you know well and love in return? Is that circle of love expanding as you meet new people? Do you give and receive love easily with persons of either sex? Is there someone special with whom you share the kind of sex life you desire?

Above all, do you love yourself? Do you *like* yourself, totally and feel comfortable with who you are and how you live? Or are you in conflict with yourself, liking yourself some of the time while not liking yourself the rest of the time? Are you able to nurture yourself with compassion and understanding when you fall short of being perfect? Do you give to yourself as well as to others?

If things are not the way you want them to be, do you know why? If you are not drawing to yourself the kind of people you want, do you know what's wrong? How many people who were important in your life five years ago are still around? How many of those who are important to you now will still be with you a year from now? Do you really enjoy whom you are with and what you do? Is your life the way you want it to be?

If it is not, do you understand why your life works this way? (If you don't know, this book may help you find out, while pointing you toward doing something about it.)

Think a moment about your answers to the questions above . . . If you are unreservedly happy with what came to mind as you read the questions, and your love life is beautiful, that's wonderful. For you life is probably a great and glorious adventure of spiritual, emotional, intellectual, and physical fulfillment. You know how to give and receive love.

If this is not your experience, then you are among the unfortunate. For you something is wrong—terribly wrong. The love you dream of never quite becomes reality. You meet, barely touch and move on, like a stone skipping across still water. Or you begin love affairs that begin well enough, perhaps even quite intensely, but eventually fizzle out, if not sooner then later. Your marriage relations aren't doing well, either. What was once the culmination of your hopes for love is becoming more and more a battle ground. Even the best marriages between "healthy" people are falling apart, either through divorce or by continuing in name only. Husbands, wives, friends, lovers, brothers, sisters, parents, and children are groping and wondering to themselves, "Whatever happened to love? Is it just a childhood fantasy?"

Certainly not. That love life you have wished for, or struggled in vain to create, is not just a dream of idealistic youth. Nor is love just a word. It really is possible to love and be loved with fulfillment, not just for a moment but for the rest of your life.

Love is not only possible, it is natural. We were created

for love and to love. Nothing is more real than love; nothing is more painful than its absence.

Compounding the problem is that love seems to be all around us. We see, hear, and read about love (or its substitutes) almost everywhere. Much of this subtle and overt stimulation helps foster an intense desire to experience love. We want love, and we want to be loved—there's no use denying it, even to ourselves.

All of which serves to heighten our disappointment and frustration at not achieving love. With all that is being written and said about love and human relationships, we are well informed on the need for love and the consequences of not attaining it. We know that we need to be more genuinely loving of ourselves and of others. We hear of it in sermons, on the radio, see it in the movies, t.v., read of it in books and magazines. The idea has been all around us for a long time. Anyone who isn't living in a cave or on a deserted island can tell you that—as the song says—what the world needs now is love.

If love is difficult to find, it is not for lack of searching. People work diligently to get love. One common way is to become attractive, spend time in places in which other searchers are found, and wait for the right person to come along. Often people do this while kidding themselves that love depends on finding the right person with an attractive mix of good qualities and a minimum of bad ones.

"If only I could find a good-looker with brains and a sense of humor," he kids himself, "it would be easy enough to love."

"If only I could find a tender man who knows how to make a living and wants to have a family (or doesn't want a family)," she kids herself, "love would be no problem."

The popular image of the ideal man and woman varies with the times. Nonetheless, the delusion behind this kind of attitude is that until we meet someone who fulfills our expectations, we have to withhold love from the world.

The variety and mobility of people in our large urban areas only perpetuates the false hopes of those who look for someone "out there" to release the love inside them. While it is true that each new day is a fresh opportunity to find that "wonderful" person who will make the dream happen, it is also true that for those who cannot love, each new day is likely to be a replay of a familiar disappointment and emptiness. Life often becomes a struggle when we start with a false assumption and then try to make it come true. This is self-deception.

Love is up to you, not *them*. If your love life is terrible, it isn't because . . . (Fill in the blank with whatever excuses you've been giving yourself: "It's hard to meet people." "I'm not good-looking enough." "I don't have enough money." "I don't like hanging around bars making phony talk." "There's nobody my type around here." "Nobody wants a divorced woman with kids," and so forth.)

While people are mistakenly looking for another person to open them to love, others are seeking love through meditation, prayer and religion. They believe that somehow God, maybe through a miracle or through one of the lesser angels, will open their hearts to love. In the Western world there has been a long line of ministers, priests, rabbis, teachers, who have barraged and admonished us with the need to love.

"God is love," they tell us. "Love thy neighbor as thyself." "Love conquers all." "God so loved the world that He gave His only begotten son," etc.

While religious experiences can be glorious, it hardly does much good for those who don't know how to love. Much of what we know as religion is preaching and admonitions, which can cause more confusion, discomfort, and guilt. After all, says the "sinner," if I won't listen to the voice of God, then I must really be hopelessly lost—and *really* unworthy of love. The result is more guilt, not more love.

The problem with religion as a path to love is that it *commands* people to act in a way that is only meaningful when done out of free choice. Love cannot be ordered. While it is possible to order people to behave *as if* they loved their neighbors, no amount of admonitions or threats will cause them to feel a love they do not feel. The secret guilt of many apparently pious persons stems from this truth. Deep within they know they don't feel the love they pretend to feel. Tragically, the guilt makes them try harder. They look at the examples of Moses, Jesus, Mohammed, Buddha, or some saintly person and attempt to be like their spiritual hero. But they can't *be* their love heroes; they can only be *like* them, which means they are imitating someone else instead of being themselves.

It is not only Christianity and Judaism that have this problem. Many have turned away from Western religion to Eastern religions, particularly Buddhism and its variants. In this time of instability, confusion, and uncertainty, gurus and other spiritual masters have considerable influence. It is possible to sit before a guru and have the experience of receiving his love, blessing, and knowledge. You can join his ashram, follow him to India and back and get daily injections of his spiritual love. This won't make you a lover, although the appearance can be convincing.

No spiritual journey, however high or enlightened, is sufficient to teach love. Like a kite in the air, the spirit may soar with the guidance of the master, but the rest of the self remains on the ground, holding the string and watching.

This is not to say that the valuable teachings of the East should be ignored. Those who wish to understand the thought and experience of the mystics should search for the truths they contain. But they should be aware that it is an illusion to think that one can learn self-love by sitting before a mystic. And remember that it isn't nearly as difficult to love God, who is perfect, as it is to love the real men and women who sit next to you while you pray or meditate.

The love of self and others takes place on the emotional level of our beings, while the love of God through prayer takes place on a spiritual plane. In the same way that people with emotional limitations sometimes overdevelop their intellects to compensate for their deficiencies, highly religious people are often struggling to make up for their emotional problems by overdeveloping their spirituality. Each of us is a non-physical Trinity of intellect, emotions, and spirit within a physical body. Thus, while it is commendable to develop your spirituality, it is a mistake to think that more and more spirituality will enable you to love yourself and others on the emotional level. A commune full of well-intentioned, highly spiritual vegetarians who have never learned to love themselves is no more loving than an apartment complex of swinging singles who poison and anesthetize themselves with alcohol and tobacco to avoid their inner pain. The appearance is highly different, but the inner reality is the same: no love.

This is not to put down communes or other experimental, unconventional living arrangements. A few communes have been successful because of the true loving nature of the persons involved. Those are the ones who love themselves selflessly and can give that love to others easily and naturally from the core of their being. Their success comes from who they are, however, not their lifestyle.

The proof is not in my argument but in your own experience. Ask yourself if finding the right person, experiencing religiosity, or meditating, or communal living has taught you to love yourself and others. If you are honest with yourself, you will see that none of these activities, however beneficial and well-intentioned, gets to the emotional problem of love.

While much of this sounds highly negative, it is by no means despairing or pessimistic. Beneath the surface of human negativity there is a perfect diamond, the essence, the real you. By removing the encrusted dirt from the diamond, the real loving self can be set free. It is our essence, our true spiritual, perfect self.

Since lovelessness is an emotional problem, many people have gone searching through the maze of psychotherapies and to the human potential movement for the solution. Many forms of therapy, using a myraid of techniques, have been devised, ranging from encounter groups to one-to-one therapy to quasi-spiritual religious disciplines. You can talk or listen, scream or be screamed at, told how to think or not to think, be stroked, doped, joked, or poked. Some of these therapies directly approach the problem of loving oneself and others— but when they do, it's usually with more admonitions and fruitless positive thinking exercises. Most are open-ended and offer no resolution; few are of lasting value.

As with other approaches, psychotherapy has its value. It is helpful in relieving symptoms, making people more aware of what they are doing and why, and helping them become better adjusted. Often, however, it leaves people with more confusion and conflict, and no more loving, than when they started.

Consider these words of a highly respected, highly experienced clinical psychologist who says it like it is:

> *I spent my whole adult life seeking an end to my inner turmoil. I got my doctorate in psychology, but didn't find my answers. I went into analysis and studied to be an analyst. I made progress, but the resolution was always elusive. I went into group*

therapy then and began experimenting to find a cure for patients and myself. I studied many new approaches, made more and more progress. I discovered Gestalt therapy and made the most dramatic progress of all. I became a Gestalt therapist myself, but still no solution. So after eighteen years of practice, I came to California still looking for a resolution to my problems . . . I've given up in despair many times and bounced back and tried again. I'm tired of just making more and more progress. I want to make it all the way.

Most professional therapists know the cause of emotional problems: the programming that children receive from their parents. But *knowing is not enough.* Therapists and their clients often gain more and more knowledge without becoming any more loving because there is a split, or lack of integration, between the emotions and the intellect. More and more information fed into the intellect only increases the tension and conflict without really changing the program. Head trips and intellectual understanding have failed.

Another way to put this is to say that you cannot *figure* your way out of an emotional problem, you must *feel* your way out. There are therapies, which deal with the deepest feeling levels and often bring some resolution of unfinished childhood business. While they may go to the cause, they tend to resolve the traumas one at a time and quite slowly. The hoped-for final resolution is rare, and they go on for years never ending the therapy.

Therapies that don't teach self-love are never finished. They cannot be. Until your cup of love is filled to overflowing, there is always something missing in your life. No matter how well things may be going, the absence of total love leaves a gaping hole in your life. Psychotherapy can and does soothe the pain around the edges and fill some of the emptiness, but those who experience it must judge for themselves whether it fills that empty space belonging to self-love.

While millions of people have searched resolutely for the secret of love, many more have not. Instead, they go through life preferring to keep their eyes covered, seeing nothing. They know they hurt, and all they want is something for the pain. For them the variety of pain killers is almost endless. Food is a common way to kill the pain. Eating more than your body needs for nutrition and health is a coverup for lovelessness. Beyond the infantile need for oral gratification, overeating bloats the stomach, which literally dulls the senses and dims the awareness of the outside world. While the body is working on digesting an excessive quantity of food, the intellect cannot think, and the emotions cannot be expressed, particularly the pained and angry emotions of lovelessness. The best cure for obesity, therefore, is learning to love yourself.

Like food, almost anything you take into your body, alcohol, cigarettes, and drugs of all kinds, can be used to kill the pain of not giving and receiving love. The difficulty in kicking the drinking, smoking, and drug habits is that these substances are not used for themselves but to prevent something even worse: the full experiencing of how excrutiatingly painful it is to live without love. People will do anything, including killing themselves with heroin, to avoid feeling that pain. It's sad but true that what is really killing the drunks, chain-smokers, and junkies is not their habits but their total lack of love for themselves and others. More the pity.

Most people are more fortunate. But not much. Instead of killing themselves to avoid the pain, they live mostly anesthetized against it. They do this by using something else as a substitute for love. It is as if they say to themselves, "Well, if I can't get love from the world I'll take all the _____ I can get." You name it and people have used it as a substitute for love. Money, sex, power, fame, material possessions, whatever.

In most of the world, money and material possessions are the most widely sought after substitutes for love, in part because people equate money with one's personal value and esteem. While almost everyone agrees that money cannot buy love, almost nobody *acts* as if he believes it. Many people seem willing to settle for an unloving life if they can surround themselves with possessions. There is certainly nothing wrong with possessions in themselves. The products of human intelligence, creativity, and labor are ours to enjoy in this life, but it is a bad bargain to sacrifice love while pursuing them.

The rich can also surround themselves with other people if they choose to, although having a lot of people around is not proof of love. Love is measured by the quality of relationships, not their quantity. In surrounding themselves with people, the rich are often lonely. There is sometimes comfort in crowds, except that in the crowd one can be lost and feel rejected. The lonely rich boy and the poor little rich girl are just as poor in the love quotient as those in the middle class and lower class who are also without love.

Unfortunately, people continue to kid themselves that if only they had a lot of money, or a lot *more* money, they would be able to get love and feel love. An old and powerful illusion dies hard. It really is an illusion, since if you think about it and look at reality, you can see that people with more money are not more loving than those without it. They are undoubtedly better able to hide their pain, since they look happier and superficially may even feel better.

People can deny the truth about love and money and struggle all their lives to "prove" a lie, but the truth doesn't go away simply by denying it. What is, is. Money buys people temporarily, and it buys the substitutes for love. The real thing is beyond price.

Work is also a common substitute for love and a way of killing the pain of not getting it. People who work hard and well can even use work to acquire a lot of the other pain-killers, such as money, power, and sex. If the world approves of the way they work, they can also kid themselves that the world "loves" them. The world may need the work they do—but that is economics, not love.

Work is also a way of avoiding love completely. The man or woman who works twelve or more hours a day can use fatigue or lack of time as excuses for avoiding love. For some people it is easier to be married to a business or career than to a person.

Weekends and vacations, too, are often filled compulsively with things to do so unloving people won't have to face how empty they feel. Travel and leisure-time industries are partially supported by the need of millions of loveless people to *do* something, *anything*, to keep from facing how bad, how thoroughly terrible, it is to live without love.

Perhaps most pathetic of all are the loners, those who live year after year with a minimum of human contact. They get up in the morning, go to their jobs, come home in the evening, eat alone, and spend the evening with a book or the television. The next day is the same. And the next. On the weekends they go out for a walk, a drive, or to a museum—

always alone, rarely talking to anyone, almost never touching or being touched.

Like the searching singles, loners have a variety of excuses for not making it with people: "I like my solitude." "I never found anyone I cared enough about." "It's too much trouble." "I'm hard to like." "I don't want to get involved." "They might ask something of me, and I hate to say no." And many more.

Behind the aloneness is fear. Avoiding other people is safer than risking even a temporary rebuff or rejection. After a few years they find a certain level of relationship with which they can cope with a minimum of hassles, and that's it. Emotionally these people go dead for the rest of their lives.

Sartre said that hell is other people, and loners seem to live as if they believed that. Actually, hell is other people only when other people are in hell. Underneath the zombie exterior of the loner is a deep longing of love that is rarely acknowledged.

For those who "know" they are unworthy of love, or who have never known love, one way to cover the pain is to deny that love exists or that it matters. These people think they are proving that love is something Madison Avenue uses to sell perfume and valentines. Or that even if love is real, nobody knows what it is. Or if we know what it is, love is inconvenient and a barrier to more important things.

This argument is somewhat more difficult to counter because on one level all of it is correct. Advertisers do use our intense desire for love to motivate us to buy their products. It is also accurate to say that love is difficult to define to everyone's satisfaction. Certainly it is correct that those who are involved in loving themselves and others may not spend as much time working and traveling alone as those who do not love.

While all of it is accurate, none of it is true. For on a deeper level those who deny love and their need for it are attempting to "prove" a lie while protecting themselves against the pain of seeing the truth of their emptiness. If love doesn't exist, then you don't have to ask for it. If you don't ask, you will never be denied. It is twisted reasoning, and it makes masochistic sense.

Love is not a barrier to anything. It is the great liberator. When you love yourself for the person you are and can give that love to others, then you have found a freedom unknown to those who remain uninvolved and unattached.

You *can* change. You can love. It is possible to relearn to love yourself and others, no matter how unloved or unloving you have been. For the very essence of your being is *love!* It's never too late or too difficult. To achieve a loving state you first need to be clear about what love is, and what it is not. Much of what looks like love is something else. In fact, people are so confused, guilty, and misinformed on the subject of love that most of them can't even talk straight about it. Not that they don't talk about love, just that most of what they say either makes no sense or makes no difference.

For example, many people think giving is love. While it is true that lovers are givers, the reverse is not necessarily true. It all depends on the motive. There is a great difference between *giving to give and giving to get.* Most of the giving we see is giving to get something in return. Giving money to charity, for example, is usually given in adherence to the Biblical admonition to be charitable in return for a place in heaven. Giving to get doesn't fill an empty cup of love. Perhaps you know the story of the man who got up in church during the annual fund raising and shouted, "I wish to give $5,000 anonymously." Although he didn't say it, he could have added, "Now will you recognize me, see me, approve me, make me feel worthy, love me?" These are the motives behind so much of charitable giving. When those who really love themselves and others give, their giving is without guilt and for no other need than that of the recipient.

Giving of ourselves comes from various other motives, many of them unloving. Self-denial and martyrdom, while serving the needs of others, is often an indirect manipulation to become "one up" on the other. It's as if the martyr were saying, "See how good I am at being good? Now will you love me?" Examples abound everywhere. A recent newspaper advice column was devoted to a letter from a woman whose husband is an alcoholic. She wrote to say how much better she felt since she joined a group for wives of alcoholics. Her husband still goes out drinking every night and still makes no time for her or the children, but she's grateful to God that she joined the group which supports her; she is able to love her martyrdom. It is OK that he does those unloving things, and they are closer than ever before. And so forth.

While this woman deserves our sympathy for her desperate situation, she is using her husband's problem to glorify herself. Secretly she is saying, "Aren't I great now? See how I put up with this awful man, and I love him, and I'm a good mother, too. I've earned some love, haven't I?"

Such martyrdom and giving to get may help explain how otherwise sensible people, both men and women, can make such one-sided marriages. They feel so worthless inside themselves that they have to "save" someone else in order to feel good about themselves. Giving to get sympathy is not love. Nor is giving to animals, while ignoring people, real love. As a rule, animal lovers are compassionate people, but there are many who prefer to love animals while turning away from relationships with people. Those who have been hurt often will not risk further rejection. Giving to their pets enables them to feel needed and loved.

Often what parents give to their children is not what it appears to be. Many people claim to be loving parents, offering as proof their many sacrifices on behalf of their children. While the sacrifices in time and money are easy enough to see, the expectation of something in return is usually kept hidden. Not until the children rebel or don't meet the parent's expectations does the truth come out. "How could they do this to us after all we did for them?" These anguished cries are the hallmark of parental giving to get, which in effect is pseudo-love.

Many people experience strong sexual attraction and mistake it for love. They get so excited around their sex object, so thoroughly turned on, that they're certain this is what they have been waiting for. To him, she is so perfect in every way, so exactly the image he has fantasied for years. It's as if his fairy godmother sent her to him. Now, he thinks, at last I have found her, and I can love freely and forever. Or anyway, for a long time. For her it's the same. He is so exciting, so strong, so manly in all the ways she has dreamed of. Now she can surrender to love and give all. Well, almost all.

Sometimes they even make it together. Sex is an exciting natural biological act, and we live in a time of great sexual freedom and openness, so why not? No particular reason, except that while the itch in your groin is powerful, and relieving it feels good, it isn't love. Particularly if the deal is giving to get; "I'll love you and be nice to you if you'll love me and be nice to me."

Part of the confusion about love and sex comes from the odd way we have of talking about sex. We say, "I want to make love," as if it were in our power to create love. We cannot make love, we can only exchange the love that already exists deep within us. We also speak of "free love" as if it were just there for the taking. In loveless sex it isn't the love that is free but the body.

The confusion between sex and love also stems from the nature of the activity. The warmth and closeness of the lover's body can trigger the memory of being at mother's breast or in father's protective arms. Often in the sex act the partners will cry out in their passion that they love each other. What they love is the moment that recalled the feeling of union with mother or feeling close to father.

This is assuming, of course, that they experienced such physical warmth during infancy. Some children, a small but nonetheless tragic number, never felt the warmth of mother's breast or body or the strength and protection of father's arms. Without these important childhood experiences of physical, emotional, and spiritual closeness it is almost impossible to experience, much less enjoy, adult sexuality. Or adult love. Those who were not fondled with tenderness as children find it all but impossible to express or receive tenderness as adults. Fortunately, total lack of physical fondling is rare. What most of us missed is the *consistent* experience of parental emotional tenderness.

This restimulation of childhood feelings during sexual intercourse helps explain how lovers can be so passionate in bed and so cold and unloving afterward. It isn't necessarily that they dislike each other except for sex. Rather, who the other person actually is doesn't matter since he/she is just a stand-in for mother or father.

What, then, happened to love? The answer is that as children we did not learn how to love. Instead, we saw our parents kidding themselves that the substitutes they accepted in place of love were the real thing. Instead of seeing the truth we saw the lie and believed it. Thus, we learned to think that love is sex, money, food, martyrdom, hard work, or poetry.

Love is a feeling and a state of being, and it comes from the spiritual essence, "the light" within ourselves. We learn to feel it by experiencing it directly in our relations with our parents during our childhood. If we experience more than enough loving during those formative years, there will be a lifelong surplus we can share with others. If we don't learn to use our ability to love during childhood, it becomes dormant. Then the things we do as adults that look like love are just play-acting. If all we know how to do is to act love, we are in for a great deal of emptiness and pain. For the act is a poor substitute for the real thing.

Love between men and women is particularly susceptible to the danger of acting out a role. Romance and sexual encounters are so much a part of popular entertainment that what most people know about love, or think they know, comes from television, movies, and books. The tragedy is that most of what is dramatic in popular love stories is not love but various kinds of manipualtion. Since heartache and catastrophe are more familiar than serene happiness, the stories most people associate with love are filled with frustration, conflict, and corruption.

There are several important conclusions to be drawn from all of this. To be a lover you must first love yourself. You cannot figure your way out of your failure to love yourself and others. Lack of self-love is like a locked cage, and intellect is not the key. You cannot just read a book full of well intentioned admonitions and stop being unloving. (You may even have picked up this book with something like that in mind.) Books cannot teach people how to love, although they are helpful in giving information and understanding. If books could teach love and how to feel it, we might have stopped with the Old Testament.

It may seem odd using a book to tell you that a book cannot make you into a lover. Yet this is the easiest way to share information with a large number of people. Although *knowing* won't solve an emotional problem, knowing that you don't know is the beginning of true knowledge. And the knowledge here can help you *find* the way.

Second, there are no tricks to the truth of self-love. Meditation, psychoanalysis, jogging, drugs, encounter, fasting, massage, you name it, none of them will make any difference in your love life until you learn to love yourself.

Third, and best of all, there *is* a way out. Despite the negativity of much of what I have said, the positive truth is there is hope for everyone. For *everyone* is loveable. You *can* learn to love yourself. Change is possible. No matter how stuck you may feel, no matter how negative your life is or has been, what you have always hoped for yourself really is possible.

While this book cannot make it happen for you, it can show you how things went wrong and what others have done to make them right again. When they are right, you will be able freely and constructively to express the love that is inherently yours.

This book shows the origin of our inability to love ourselves. Take what you can from this book while recognizing that love is more than something to read about. Once learned, it is the ultimate human experience, and the experience is yours to claim. You have but to uncover your indestructible, diamondlike, positive, loving, spiritual essence: the *Light* that is *you*.

CHAPTER II

HOW CHILDREN
ADOPT THEIR PARENTS

Children have it rough. Whether rich or poor, in large families or small, all children live in a world they did not create, run by rules they did not make. From their point of view their lives are controlled by big, powerful people who are often inconsistent, illogical, hypocritical, frightening, cold, unloving, and, in some cases, even brutal and violent.

Children experience the unpredictability of mother's and father's love. They feel as if they are always on probation, always having to prove themselves. Before parents teach them not to recognize it, children are also aware of the difference between the real love they need and the play-acting that often substitutes for the real thing. So many don't have the parents he or she deserves.

I am aware that these are hard truths to confront. However clearly we see the flaws in our parents, we nonetheless want to believe that they loved us. Many people know they are still angry over some of the things their parents did and yet they have achieved a modicum of compassion and understanding for them. Many of us also intellectually realize that if we had it hard as kids, our parents may have had it even harder when they were children. We therefore tend to cherish our happier childhood memories while trying to forgive and forget the bad ones. Nevertheless, only by re-experiencing the entire truth about our parents can we establish a basis for true compassion and love for them.

Except for child abusers, most parents do not deliberately mistreat or harm their children. In the adult world we do the best we can in the face of our human failings and the stresses of making our way in life. Almost everyone knows that he or she has good days, bad days, and an occasional day that is best forgotten. As adults we struggle to learn to live with these ups and downs of ourselves and others.

Children live in a different world. Children have no choice but to believe that their parents and other adults always know what they are doing. Adults own and run the world, don't they? Therefore, in whatever way a child sees his parents treating him, he assumes it is intentional and right, which can be confusing. After all, how can these people who (usually) say they love him, intentionally treat him so harshly and unlovingly? Most children at one time or another have said to themselves something like, "They say they love me but . . . "

If you are like most people, you can remember times in your first five years when you were punished unjustly or excessively, and you retreated to a private place to nurse your hurt or angry feelings. Perhaps, while crying bitter tears, you decided that these people you lived with were not your real parents. You may even have had a fantasy explanation for the inconsistency; maybe there was a mixup at the hospital; or you thought when your parents went on vacation, they were kidnaped or their parents were taken over by beings from outer space. Some children think they were adopted and that someday their real parents will return to claim (or rescue) them and give them the love and protection they yearn for and know are rightfully theirs. Children will even ask if they are adopted, much to the consternation or amusement of their parents. People have told me they secretly went looking for their adoption papers in their parents' closets and drawers.

In fact, the overwhelming reality of our emotional lives is exactly the opposite. It is *we* who adopt our parents. We emulate our parents, and in so doing we adopt their positive and *negative* traits in return for both their positive and *negative attention*. Little boys try to strut like their fathers; little girls try to sit like their mothers. Almost every child at some time or other says or thinks, "I'm going to be like Daddy (or Mommy) when I grow up."

Parents even tend to encourage the imitation by laughing approvingly at a child's attempts to be grown-up. They enjoy the aping if it is positive. Sometimes they even enjoy it when it's negative. When children are playing house, for example, if the little girl scolds the "late" little boy the way mother scolds father when he's late for dinner, and the little boy imitates father's sheepish withdrawal behind the newspaper, the parents may laugh at the recognition of a common household drama.

But if it is humorous to the parents, it is deadly serious to a child. He imitates them and adopts their traits to "get" their love and approval, which he desperately needs to sustain himself. This pattern is so common that we have a number of sayings that reflect it: "Like father, like son;" "The apple doesn't fall far from the tree;" and so forth. Behind these sayings is often the *mistaken assumption* that children inherit their emotional similarity to their parents. On the contrary, children become like their parents by adopting the traits they see displayed in daily life, and this is not genetic. Children react positively or negatively to the actions of those in charge of their upbringing. It is the negative reactions which cause neurotic behavioral patterns.

The positive qualities which please and the negative qualities which annoy the parents are both adopted by children. Adopting the negative traits is where the real problems begin. If mother is fearful, the child learns not to take risks. Or if father is unemotional, the child learns not to show his feelings. When mother doesn't think much, the child learns not to solve problems. When father is a procrastinator, the child learns to be late most of the time. If mother and father each have the same negative trait, then the child gets a double dose of negativity.

Everyone possesses positivity, no matter how negatively he or she behaves. We aren't dwelling here on positivity because this is a book about problems, and the positive traits are not a problem for people *unless* they rebel against them. This will be discussed later.

The most negative trait possible is the inability to love oneself and others. If our parents did not know how to love themselves and others, they could not teach us how to give and receive love. Our parents' failure to teach us to love ourselves and others (including even them!) is the emotional cancer of our lives. Almost the entire catalogue of human misery and misfortune can be traced directly or indirectly to this "disease." If lovelessness can be linked to a cancer, then the "virus" that causes it is *negative* love. (Although I coined this Quadrinity Process expression in 1967, the concept has been known but largely ignored for many years.)

The negative love syndrome is the key to all neurotic, negative behavior patterns, especially the inability to love. When one adopts the negative traits, moods, or admonitions (silent or overt) of either or both parents, one relates to them in negative love. It is illogical logic, nonsensical sense, and insane sanity, yet the pursuit of the love they never received in childhood is the reason people persist in behaving in these destructive patterns. "See, Mom and Dad, if I am just like you, will you love me?" is the ongoing subliminal query.

Although adopting our parents' negative traits affects our ability to love, it is not limited to that one area. The adoption includes literally hundreds of traits, both important and trivial, covering every facet of our being. The negative love syndrome is the single most destructive force in marriage, sexuality, work, health, and play. There is no area of our lives that is unaffected by the example our parents set for us and the way we continue to be affected by it.

If you wish to see this for yourself in your own life, take a moment to quietly sit back and relax. Recall your mother during childhood. Picture her in a familiar room, perhaps the living room or the kitchen. See her doing or saying something typical that particularly annoyed you. Perhaps she nagged about insignificant things or was stingy with praise. It need not be something she did with you, although it may be. The point is to see something about her that was negative. (You do recognize that your parents weren't perfect?) Take a moment now to visualize one or two other scenes of your mother doing or saying something that you did not like when you were a child. It often helps to close your eyes while doing this. Experience it now.

After visualizing a few of mother's negative traits, do the same with your father. See him doing or saying something characteristic of him that made you unhappy or uncomfortable when you were a child. For example, he may have disciplined you harshly or unfairly, or showed no interest in the things that mattered to you. If you are defensive, you may have difficulty seeing anything negative about your father or your mother, yet bear in mind that even the best parents are not without some negative qualities. When you have envision-ed two or three negative traits for each parent (or their surrogates*), make a note of them.

Now take a gentle and honest look at yourself. How do your father's and mother's negative qualities express them-selves in you? Have you become like them? Are their flaws now *your* flaws? If your mother nagged and carped at others over little things, do you do it, too? Do you have the same difficulty she had in complimenting others when they do a good job? Are you like your father in overreacting to other people's failings or mistakes? Do you have little enthusiasm for the things that excite others, just like your father? What-ever their negativities, your parents are now part of you. Having made this discovery, *you must wonder* why you ex-hibit the patterns and traits that you dislike in your parents.

If you have difficulty in deciding whether you adopted a trait you disliked in your mother or father, consider asking someone who knows you well and can be objective about you. Most people need some help seeing the things about themselves they dislike.

Not only do we adopt both the positive and negative traits of our parents, we do it for the same extremely important reason: We want their love and approval. To a child, becom-ing like his mother and father appears to be the way to gain that love. However, if mother and father do not know how to give and receive selfless love, it won't work for the child. Imitating them will not gain him real love, only its pale sub-stitutes. For example, if mother is meddlesome and pushy, she probably won't respond lovingly when she is on the re-ceiving end of this trait from her own child. Parents may want their children to become like them, but they don't enjoy having their own negativities mirrored back to them. Instead of positive, loving attention, which nurtures, the child will receive negative attention, which hurts. When his parents punish him for doing what they are guilty of, he may, with justification, say, "But that's what *you* do, Mommy." Or, "But Daddy, *you* do it." This will incite the parents even

---

*If your natural parents didn't raise you, then substitute the person or persons who assumed parental responsibility for you.

more, and they will take their self-anger out on their child. The child may wind up with a double dose of anger for mir-roring his parents, while getting lost in confusion: "How come it's all right for Mommy and Daddy, and it's not all right for me?" When a child is chastised for doing what his parents do, the result is tremendous insecurity, instability, and confusion.

Worse still, if mother and father do not know how to love themselves and others, they cannot exhibit the positive trait of love as a model for their children to adopt. Instead, they show the negative trait of inability to demonstrate affection and love which children must adopt along with all the other negative traits they see, hear, and feel.

If father and mother did not really love *each other,* then their children will have difficulty maintaining loving relation-ships. This is a real problem for many. We pursue the love our parents did not know how to give and become unloving in spite of our quest for love.

When I was growing up, the word "love" was never used in our home. It was almost like a dirty word. My mother would say, "What is love? It doesn't exist." I learned to believe that in my early years. It took me many years before I could even say the word, much less understand it and give it meaning. Love didn't exist for my mother, so for many years it didn't exist for me.

To see if this is true in your own life, again recall your mother. How was her love life? Did she have warm, loving people around her? Was she able to exchange love freely with persons of both sexes, with her own parents, brothers and sisters? Did she have the kind of sex life she deeply wanted? Did she love herself and give to herself as well as to others? If she is still alive, what is her love life like right now?

Do the same with your father. How was his love life? Did people know him well and love him? Did he get to know others well and love them in return? How did he relate to his family? Did he have the kind of sex life he deeply wanted? Did he love himself and treat himself as well as he treated others? If he is still alive, what is his love life like right now?

After looking closely at your parents and their love life, compare it with your own. If you are like most people, your love life is not much different from that of your parents. (Or perhaps your love life is different from your parents', and it is taking a great deal of effort and energy to pretend to be the loving person your parents were not.) The point is that the quality of your life is no coincidence. You learned, or more likely did not learn, how to love yourself and others by following your parents' example. The inability to love oneself and others is negative love at its worst. Those who do not love have adopted this negative trait from their parents in exchange for pseudo-love, which is acting a role rather than having a genuine experience. It may hurt us and make poor sense, yet almost no child dares (or knows how to) rise above the emotional level of his parents.

Thus, "Whatever happened to love?" is that it was corrupted inadvertently or advertently by your parents. Whether they did it intentionally or unintentionally is unimportant. Good intentions do not change the facts. If your mother and father did not know how to love themselves and others, they *could not teach* you how to love!

People who had cold, unloving parents have no difficulty understanding this. If your father got drunk and beat the hell out of you and your mother, you already know that he didn't love you. Some of you may be offended because you feel your parents were good, loving people. You may refuse to believe that your parents could have harmed you intentionally. I agree that most parents mean only well for their children. Yet, if you will take off the blinders that your parents put on you, you may discover that your childhood was not as loving as you thought and that your parents, no matter how well-meaning, were the source of your feelings of being unloveable.

Be honest again; take a clear look at your love life. If your parents were good, loving people, then why aren't you totally loving of yourself and others? How is it that you failed to learn the lesson of love they offered you? What we become is no accident. If we didn't learn love, it is because they didn't teach us how!

The following is an excerpt from the writing of a young man beginning to see clearly his negative love relationship with his father and its continuing impact on his love life:

> *I was afraid of his anger, awed by his pseudo-power, and emulated him in every way possible. He quickly learned the effectiveness of the power*

he had over me and would use that power to dis-
cipline me by saying something like, "If you want
to be a man like Dad, you'll have to do it this way."
He was concerned that I should meet his expecta-
tions when we were together around people. If he
was pleased with me, he would call me "Bud,"
which was short for "Buddy." If he was displeased,
he would call me "Jim" and make some connection
between my actions and my mother's personality.
I would do anything within my power to sustain
the "Bud" level of communication with him . . . He
would suggest to me that he knew that it was diffi-
cult to relate to women because they were inferior,
but that I should placate them (my mother and
sisters), as that would make conditions easier for
both him and me, while at the same time it would
satisfy the "silly" women . . . Now I find myself
distrusting women and putting them down, and I
can't maintain a relationship . . . I'm only com-
fortable in the presence of other men, but even
then I'm not happy. I'm cold and confused and
lonely. I don't know who I am or what to
believe . . . and I don't even know how to smile.
I'm as joyless and wooden as he was.

Jim certainly became the "Buddy" his father wanted him
to be to his own devastation. Girls, too, must become the
women their mothers modeled. A young woman, Jean, wrote
the following:

My mother treated my father with blatant dis-
respect. Her resentment was very open . . . she
would insult him and make fun of him in public,
accusing him of being lazy. My father would in-
sult back, threaten to leave her and then go off on
a bender.

During the course of her Process she wrote a distraught
letter concerning her current problems with her husband:

I have been arguing with my husband about his
laziness. I want to go to work to earn some money

and he wants me to stay home and clean house.
He is also threatening to leave me because I am
too outspoken and not submissive enough.

She had a husband she could put down, just as her mother did; clearly the negative love syndrome in operation.

These two anguished people are each relating to their parents (Jim to his father, Jean to her mother), with total negative love. Each is perfectly emulating the traits from the parent of the same sex, becoming "father's little boy" and "mother's little girl." It does not lead to a happy life, but as children, we have little choice. When children don't get the real love and acceptance they need, they find it necessary to *do something* to gain mother's or father's attention or pseudo-love. When genuine love isn't available, children have to settle for false, negative love. Then at least mother and father know they exist.

The interaction between parents and children is hardly this simple, of course. Children adopt negative traits from both parents without becoming a carbon copy of either one. In many areas they try to rebel against the parental traits. The freewheeling, hell-raising daughter of the pious minister is a classic example of a child rebelling against parental example. Yet, however successful the rebellion may be on the surface, it is not what it appears to be. Inside this kind of rebellious person there is usually deep remorse and inner frustration over the failure of the rebellion to substitute for the real love she never got from her father. Rebellion always leads to conflict and guilt.

Rebellion also shows itself in less serious ways. A woman client reported that she was a good housekeeper like her mother. Since I knew the client to be quite rebellious, I probed a bit.

"You mean every room in your house is neat?" I asked. "All your drawers, too?"

"Yes," she said. "Every room." She paused and then said, "Except the sewing room. That's always a mess. But that's just my sewing room."

"Nonsense," I replied. "You may think you're keeping house mother's way, but you're allowing yourself a space to be sloppy, which is rebellion against your mother's neatness. You must be frustrated and in conflict about the appearance of your sewing room."

She thought about it a moment and then said, "You know, you're right, Bob. I always feel uncomfortable with the way that room looks. I guess I do have a conflict over her neatness."

Every rebellious child is raging inside over his parents' failure to show him the love he desperately needs and wants. What he is angry about is that he doesn't *feel* loved despite the loving words he may hear. Since it is usually unsafe and often ineffective for a child to express his anger directly, the anger takes on disguises. Instead of screaming, "No! You can't make me!" the covert angry child learns to "get even" by doing poorly in school, ignoring the rules at home, or whatever. Secretly the angry, emotional child is saying, "Nyaah, nyaah. I'll show you, bad mother and father. You want me to do it your way, but I won't. *You'll* be sorry, and if I can't get your positive attention, I will make you notice me with negative attention." Self-destructive problems of adulthood can be traced to the rebellion of a child who is still holding on to the anger with mother and father.

Frequently a child is angry, for example, over the competition with his brothers and sisters for the attention and approval of mother and father. Children often learn early that there is not enough love to go around. If an older brother gets positive attention for being highly intelligent and a good student, the younger one may decide he cannot compete with his brother and will rebel by *pretending* to be stupid and lazy. More the pity; he soon believes that his pretense is real. By rebelling in this destructive way he gains the negative attention of one or both parents. If this sounds masochistic and illogical, it is. Positive love makes more sense and feels better than negative love and negative attention. Yet, when a child sees that only negative attention is available from his parents, he will choose it over *no* attention at all. Better something than nothing.

Rebellion always leads to inner conflict. This results in the seesaw feeling we experience when there are competing messages inside our heads. Ask yourself how often you have told yourself you need to behave differently in order to enhance your life. And you really intend to change because you know it's right. You assume responsibility and then, unfortunately, you wind up back in the same boat while feeling frustrated over your failure to change. This emotional conflict also evinces itself when you sometimes act one way and other times another, never really feeling good about either. In many ways our most difficult problems come when we're struggling with conflict as a result of rebelling against our parents. All inner conflict stems from the negative love we adopted from our parents and our fruitless attempts to rebel against it.

Conflict has several different sources. If a child receives competing messages from mother and father, he may be torn apart trying to please both. For example, if father is a spendthrift and mother hates to spend money, the child is doomed to lose either way. If he expresses negative love for father by spending wildly, he will be rebelling against mother, causing conflict. If he saves his money, expressing negative love for mother, he will be rebelling against father's trait, causing another conflict. He may buy the most expensive equipment for his hobby while eating only in the cheapest restaurants he can find. By doing both he relates to *both* parents in the pattern of negative love. He can't win—but to lose.

There is a subtle irony in this example. Father's spending and mother's saving may balance the marriage financially. However, what may be a workable arrangement for a husband and wife can be a hidden but agonizing source of conflict and guilt for their children.

Conflict arises because of competing messages of the intellect and the emotions. The rebellious emotional child within us may be doing something our intellect knows is dangerous or destructive. Such destructive behaviors as cigarette smoking, alcoholism, overeating, and drug addiction are common sources of conflict. Our intellects tell most of us that these things are damaging and life threatening, yet the rebellious child within says something like, "Try and stop me, Mother or Father! I'll show *you*." (This conflict between the intellect and the emotions is the reason most attempts to permanently solve addiction are ineffective. No amount of information or encouragement is powerful enough to counter the force of our angry, rebellious child underneath the veneer of our intellect. In the most extreme cases even the fear of untimely death is not a strong enough deterrent.)

Jane was the child of a handsome, yet sadistic father and a pretty, masochistic mother. During her childhood the only attention she received from him was an almost daily beating.

While hitting her, he would scream, "Take that! Take that! Take that!" In terror and pain she would cry, "Don't, Daddy! Don't Daddy! Don't!" Since any attention is better than being ignored, she masochistically learned to love the negative attention she was getting from Daddy. The hidden emotional, unexpressed justification was, "At least Daddy sees me. I have contact with him." During her childhood years the only physical touching between them were these painful, humiliating beatings. She was often witness to her mother's painful beatings.

With the mother and father she had, it was almost inevitable that as an adult she would express her negative love for them by marrying a handsome man who, like her father, was a sadist. Whenever her husband beat her, the negative emotional child within her silently cried out to her father, "See, Daddy? I'm not being disloyal to you. The man I married is beating me up just like you did me and Mommy. Now will you love me, Daddy?"

And from deep within she plaintively and silently cried out to her mother, "I didn't outdo you. My man's beating me up just the way Daddy beat you up. I'm not disloyal to you and your values. I'm just the same as you. I haven't risen above you. Now will you love me, Mommy, and feel sorry for me?"

The power behind this pathetic pattern was her childhood fear that in outdoing her parents she would not be loyal to them and thus become unworthy of their love. Finally, however, she did rebel and divorce her sadist husband.

For her second husband she chose a kind, thoughtful, loving man. While this appeared to be a successful rebellion, it was not. He was a good husband to her, yet she was miserable. She would sob to me, "He is so good, Bob, but I can't love him." You see, she had dared to rebel against Daddy and was paying the price. Her depression was caused in her frustrating conflict between negative love for her father and her attempt to rebel against him. The negative child within, to defend itself against the rebellious act, then silently cried out to her parents, "See Daddy, I'm still loyal to you because I'm not really loving this good man even though I rebelled and married him. I haven't totally deserted you, Daddy. And, Mommy, I haven't outdone you. I rebelled, Mommy, but I'm not letting him love me. See, I'm not getting any more love than you did. Now will you love me?"

The story of Jane's unhappy marriages, although somewhat extreme, shows several important aspects of negative love and its variants, rebellion and conflict. Her destructive negative love for her father and mother remain with her into adulthood and determined her choice of a husband. Second, while her intellect may have known that the first husband was a poor choice, her negative emotional child was the part of her that made the decision. Unfortunately, her negative emotional child was also in control during her second marriage. While her situation may have appeared to improve, it was not better on the emotional level. Third, her conflict was what prevented her from accepting the love her intellect knew was available in the second marriage. The intellect is a mere speck on the ocean of emotion. Her negative love patterns were so powerful she was unable to break them by herself. This is the horror of negative love.

Child abuse is pure unadulterated negative love. Jane did not choose to inflict the sadistic treatment she received from her father's hand onto her children. She chose to take it onto herself. However, unfortunately, many others who were victims of child abuse choose as parents to relate in like fashion to their children by adopting the sadistic trait. Parents who are compulsively locked into their negative behavior pattern are guilty and yet emotionally not to be blamed. They are crippled by the devastating negative love syndrome. Usually, the parents, having emotionally inflicted beatings on the children, are filled with remorse. They may even think that the beating was a responsible action but make affirmations and resolutions to exercise self-control in the future. Strong-willed people may even succeed for a while, yet the suppressed power of negative love eventually explodes and wins out in the end, and the child loses.

Jane adopted her negative love patterns from both parents. However, the lack of one parent does not necessarily simplify or ease the situation. A missing parent has an enormous influence, as witnessed in the story of Ellen. Her father deserted her and her mother when she was four years old. Her mother spent the next forty years alone and lonely, rejecting any possibility of male friendship, companionship, or love.

Ellen blamed her mother for her father's flight and became bitterly hostile and angry. She spent her adult life in shallow, brief marriages with a succession of men from whom she wanted the love her missing father took with him. When single, she was desperate to be married. This was rebellion against her mother. Yet shortly after each wedding she began to find fault with the current relationship. She would *not allow* any man to give her the love her father did not give her. Stuck as she was in the resulting conflict, she was miserable when she was married and miserable when she was divorced. She clung to each marriage until she could stand it no longer and then would leave. Finally, in her fifties, she ceased her rebellion and recognized that she could not be content in a loving relationship with a man. For this would have been outdoing mother. Worn out by the conflict resulting from rebelling against her mother, she gave up and settled for spending the rest of her life alone, *just like mother*, and in total negative love to her.

Like many people with emotional problems, Jane and Ellen were unaware of how their troubles stemmed from negative love patterns. In their ignorance they sincerely believed their acts of rebellion would bring them greater happiness and love. It is this common but mistaken belief that one's acts of rebellion will lead to something better that adds poignancy to the tragedy of the negative love relationship with parents.

In addition to their traits and moods, children also adopt their parents' negative admonitions, both spoken and unspoken. "You're not good enough" is so frequent an admonition that it is almost universal. Children who live with criticism stand little chance of learning to love themselves. A forty-five-year-old doctor, highly competent and respected in his profession, recalled this childhood scene as one of many examples of his mother's devastating criticisms:

> *I was not quite five years old. I asked my mother if I could put stamps on her letters. I put them on crooked—I'd seen mail come to the house with stamps on crooked and thought that was the way people put stamps on letters. Later, she saw the letters with crooked stamps and exploded into anger. "Why didn't you put them on straight? They look terrible. I'm ashamed to send them out. You're a bad boy! Naughty!" I felt crushed. I thought I*

was doing the right thing, but she acted like I was stupid and had done a bad thing on purpose. My stomach felt tight and hurt.

While this man obeyed his parents' admonition to become a doctor, he also adopted his mother's negative admonitions. He was bright and hard-working, yet he carried into adulthood the terrible doubts about his competence instilled by his mother's frequent criticisms. In medical school he nervously crammed for examinations even when he was thoroughly prepared. In his later medical practice he often called in specialists to confirm diagnoses he already knew were correct. He never learned to trust himself because he was consumed with the self-doubt programmed by his mother.

Besides the obvious spoken admonitions, parents also give their children powerful silent admonitions. Usually the silent admonition comes as the companion to a more innocent spoken one. For example, the spoken admonition, "Mind your manners," carries with it the unstated implication, "Your manners are not good," or "If I don't remind you all the time, you'll forget." Children get the real message even when nothing is said.

Here is how a forty-year-old minister described one of his childhood experiences with the silent admonition not to express warmth physically: "I remember when going to bed, I wanted mother to come in and hug me good night, but she'd only come as far as the door and say, 'Good night. Don't forget to say your prayers,' as she turned out the light. I'd lay there hating her and plotting ways to get even because she didn't care enough to come in and give me a hug!"

Although his mother may not have realized it, she was teaching her son something more influential in his life than just to say his prayers at night. He adopted both her spoken admonition to pray and the even more powerful silent admonition not to touch those who were dear to him. As a parent himself, he found it almost impossible to embrace his children, and they learned from him the same lesson he learned from his mother.

Not all admonitions are given or received so quietly as were those of the minister's mother. Sometimes they are part of harsh disciplining. A twenty-eight-year-old client told me of such an incident from when he was four years old:

My mother was standing at the front door talk-
ing to the mailman and I was playing on the floor.
I was directly underneath her and looked up, cur-
iously, under her dress. This so enraged her that
she immediately pulled me up and slapped and
scolded me in front of this stranger. The pain and
embarrassment and guilt were so great that it most
surely laid a foundation for my unease with women
and sex.

So deeply did this man take into himself the admonition
that it is wicked to look at a woman's body, that after ten
years of marriage he still cannot bring himself to watch his
wife undress. He knows intellectually that there is nothing
wrong with seeing her naked and that it ought to please and
excite him. But his emotional programming overwhelms his
present-day knowledge, and he responds to the sight of his
wife's body with the fear and shame his mother drove into
him. Ergo, a terrible sex life.

Parental acts of omission during childhood create as many
problems as acts of commission. The things parents do not
do and do not say are equally effective in creating negative
childhood programs. For example, if a child does not see his
father demonstrating love and affection for his mother, and
does not see mother asking for it, he will learn to be undemonstrative. Later, in adult life, when he is expected to
show love he may find the best he can do is to falsely act out
a role. This sort of pretending is especially common in love
and sexual relations. People who have not learned to feel
love for others are expected to act as if they did. As earlier
pointed out, books and movies are often used to teach people
how to play the part of the lover without actually feeling it.
If love affairs, marriages, even friendships, have an empty and
incomplete feeling to them, it is often because there is little
or no genuinely warm feeling below the surface action. To
reiterate: to be real, love must be learned and experienced in
childhood.

Another common act of omission that has severely damaging consequences is simply for the parents to be unavailable
for the child. When the parents are usually so busy with their
own interests and activities that the child feels they do not
really see or hear him, he learns to adopt the belief, "I don't

matter to others. I am unimportant and unworthy." A divorced mother who adopted this silent admonition recalled this scene as typical of her childhood:

> *When I was two, I toddled up to my mother and tugged at her skirt to get her attention. She brushed me away, saying that she was busy. I always remember her as busy. I remember her rushing around pell-mell at breakneck speed, with millions of little errands and chores she felt she had to do. The mornings were a total rush. She wanted everyone dressed and fed in the narrow time limits she kept. She was always anxious that her time plan wouldn't be kept—that one of the kids would do something spontaneous and she wouldn't get everything done in just the way she wanted.*

From her busy mother she learned to be a busy, harried mother herself. She, too, ran around, keeping schedules and being short-tempered with her children while getting angry with herself because she was behaving like her mother. She was also frustrated because she didn't know what to do about it. The heavy demands on her time and energy in running a household with no husband are compounded tragically by her emotional need to emulate her mother.

In addition to the effect of acts of omission, it is important to realize that the negative love programming need not include severe trauma or family uproar. A quiet household is not necessarily a loving one. In fact, children of parents who fought often find it easier to express their feelings than children of those who kept a false peace. The programming and adopting of parents' traits, moods, and admonitions goes on day after day, quietly, in many cases with little or no awareness of what is happening. Often it isn't until people compare their childhood recollections with others that they consciously realize how many important things were missing from their zombie-like home life.

To summarize, children adopt their parents' negativities in return for pseudo-love, which serves as an inadequate substitute for real love. When children rebel against their parents, they experience conflict and anxiety, which block the natural flow of love. The almost universal inability to love is the most destructive effect of negative love.

This then is the basic structure of the negative love concept, but in life it is even more complex than so far described. Children of the same parents do not turn out the same. Brothers and sisters, even twins, are quite individualistic and diverse. There are several reasons for this. The family system changes as time passes. New parents with only one child are different from the parents they become after a second or third child. Also, as the family changes, the situation facing each new child alters, how much so depending on how much the family itself has changed. There is a great difference between a three-person household consisting of mother, father, and a three-year-old, and a four-person household consisting of the same mother, no father, and three children ages eight, five, and two. Thus, the negative love programming of each child can change during the years from embryo to puberty, and the programming of all the children is rarely similar.

On the other hand, even when the programming changes little from one child to the next, children who are close in age do not usually respond to it in the same way. The pattern of the older, goody-goody child and the younger, rebellious child is a common one. Each child experiences basically the same set of traits, moods, and admonitions from mother and father, yet they respond differently. If the older child so closely fits the parents' expectations that he receives large amounts of positive attention from both mother and father, the younger may view the three as an unbreakable triangle. If insufficient positive attention appears to be available, the usual recourse is to rebel and gain the parents' negative attention. The first child is responding to the programming with total negative love, while the second is responding with rebellion. It is also true that if the older son feels displaced by the younger, to whom mother and father are giving all the positive attention, the older may be the one to rebel and the younger becomes the goody-goody.

Even when children respond to the programming in the same basic manner, that is, compliance or rebellion, the response can take different forms. Children do not necessarily rebel in the same way. Consider the case of John and his two sons, John, Jr., and Peter. In the 1940s and early 1950s John was a dedicated Communist, which by then was not only unfashionable but dangerously illegal. To his associates in the party he seemed a strong, loving man who was always speaking, conspiring, and pouring his energy into the movement for the social change he was convinced was vital to the welfare of the entire world. Meanwhile, his family lived in poverty and saw little of him since everything beyond necessities went for the benefit of his cause (and to gain attention).

In his later years John became deeply disillusioned about the possibility of social change. As a result he suffered from devastating insomnia and took heavier and heavier doses of sleeping pills to control it. Eventually his health failed, and he died of a drug overdose. John, Jr., was twelve, Peter was ten when their father died.

How each responded to the programming of their father reveals the subtle complexity of negative love and its variants, rebellion and conflict. Both rebelled by taking no interest in politics or the welfare of others. John, Jr., rebelled against his father's poverty and concern for the "oppressed workers" and strove compulsively to join the Capitalist financiers against whom his father fought. Ignoring his wife and children (negative love), he became obsessed with making money (rebellion). While it appeared he would achieve his financial goal, the conflict he experienced because of his rebellion, and the destruction of his family life, left him suffering from nervous anxiety, which kept him awake night after night. (Negative love to daddy.)

Peter, too, rebelled against his father's social example. However, he adopted his father's drug dependency, and even became a dealer in heroin. Because of his conflict over his rebellion, he avoided succeeding (as his father did) by being careless at the wrong times, and spent several years in jail.

As children, Peter and John, Jr., admired their dedicated father but hated him for destroying himself and abandoning them. In their anger and frustration, they each rebelled against his social concern and pseudo-love of others by pursuing purely selfish goals, although in radically different styles—yet emotionally they were each stuck in rebellion and conflict.

With negative love, nothing is quite as it seems to be. The so-called ideal child, for example, can be the delight of his parents for a while. Often a perfectly compliant child will "go crazy" with rebellion as he enters puberty. While it is tempting for parents to dismiss it as "a phase he's going through" or the result of hormonal changes, there is often much more involved. The ideal child is buying mother's and father's love, but the pressure he feels is overwhelming. He experiences the frustration of always doing things their way while never receiving the real love that is the promised reward for being "good." As his contact with the outside world increases, he becomes aware that others live without having to meet the impossible expectations he faces at home. A child understands justice even if he doesn't see it at home, and the idea that others are "getting away with it" while he isn't can produce overpowering rage and pain.

It may take longer than the first thirteen years for the pressure to build and burst. If the pressure builds more slowly, or the "child" has more stamina to withstand it, the upheaval may not come until the late thirties or early forties. Sooner or later there comes a time for most people when they no longer will compliantly feed negative love nickels into mother's and father's slot machine, especially if the "jackpot" never comes or the infrequent payoff is in wooden nickels of pseudo-love.

Some of you people find much or all of what I am saying unbelievable or offensive. Those who have voiced their objections often say something like, "What you're saying may apply to certain kinds of unfortunate people, but it doesn't apply to me. My parents were deeply in love with each other, and they were wonderful to us children. They were happy all their married lives and raised a beautiful family."

Hopefully so. After all, there are those who do know how to love themselves and others selflessly and without any hangups. Maybe your parents were one of them. If so, you are correct. This doesn't apply to you. One way to test this, however, is to see how *you* turned out. If your parents were really among those who love truly, they would have been able to fill your cup of love and send you into the world prepared to share that love with others. Which brings us back to the key question: How's your love life? If your love life isn't as "perfect" as that of your parents, what went wrong? Either they did or did not teach you how to create and maintain a satisfactory love life. One simply cannot live day after day for the first thirteen years of life experiencing a loving relationship with one's parents and then "somehow" fail to learn how to do the same for oneself. That idea doesn't make sense.

At the same time I can't accept the argument that loving parents sometimes produce an unloving child. For a number of reasons children often don't see clearly what is going on between their parents. If mother and father are each living under their own negative love admonitions to keep the peace by not showing their angry or hurt feelings, particularly at home, the pseudo-love at the dinner table may actually fool the children. This sort of charade is particularly successful if the children also receive a negative love admonition to invalidate their own perceptions and intuitions. The children may end up confused and guilty over their inability as adults to love the way they thought mother and father did. At the same time, mother and father may wonder themselves how the kids could have "gone wrong."

A common kind of false loving marriage is one between a father-type husband and a daughter-type wife. They come together and are compatible because of their complementary dependency needs. It can survive as long as Big Daddy takes care of his Little Girl, and neither of them wants to change it. While this may be a "workable" arrangement, it is not a mature love between two adults. Mature love is what children need to see and experience in order to achieve it in their own adulthood.

There are seemingly loving marriages that nonetheless produce children who cannot love. If mother's and father's love for each other is inflexible and exclusive, there may be no room for a child to share with them. If the child sees his mother and father giving love to each other while ignoring him, he may walk away and reject them because he himself *feels* rejected. Later, the parents may wonder why he won't respond when they want to give him love. It is because earlier they didn't spread out their love to include him in its protective, comforting warmth. No matter what is going on between the parents, if the circle of love isn't open to their children, the next generation will have little demonstrative love for themselves or others.

A child may also learn to be unloving if his father sees him as competition for the love and attention of his mother. If this immature father sends his child the silent admonition, "Get lost, kid," the child may have no choice but to withdraw, which expresses his negative love for Daddy. Further, if mother's silent admonition is the opposite, "Don't leave me," the child may bounce back and forth like a football. No matter which admonition he adopts, he will find himself in rebellion against one of his parents, thus leading to constant, debilitating conflict.

Both rebellion and the resulting conflict originate in the negative love patterns. Some people, though, have difficulty accepting my choice of words. "How can love be negative?" they ask. "Love just is. What you describe is certainly negative, but it isn't love."

When you emulate mother's and father's positive qualities because you admire and love them and want to be like them, the result is positive. (If mother and father were charitable, for example, they may have taught you the positive trait of giving lovingly in order to give.) On the other hand, when people emulate the bad traits of mother and father in attempting to gain their "love," the result is the spectrum of human misery, degradation, and destruction. Our innate spiritual diamondlike love is then covered with the negative traits and patterns of mother and father. The "crud" on top of our perfect spiritual self is the negativity we adopted, which in turn changes our innately perfect love to neurotic love.

The case of an unrequited love also shows the positive and negative aspects of love. When the positive love we feel for another is not returned, we hurt with the pain of rejection and misery. (Some people have said of this kind of love, "It hurts real good.") While the feeling of love is overwhelmingly beautiful when you want to give it to someone, it is also overwhelmingly devastating when not returned. Often people don't want to be positively loved and accepted, although they may not fully be aware of this. Many people feel that love is too good for them, without realizing that if their love relationships are better than their parents' were they will be outdoing them. One of the most powerful of the parental silent admonitions is, "Don't outdo me."

Some people argue with the idea of negative love by asserting that each of us has free will and that we have no one to blame for our troubles but ourselves. Yet, though we tell ourselves we have free will and control over our destinies, for most of us most of the time, autonomy is an illusion. Instead, what we do is replay the programming laid down for us by our parents during our childhood. Those who insist on their own autonomy should be aware that an important part of the program is to be unaware that it is a program. Parents tell their children the lie that they are free agents and then order them to believe it.

Some people who wish to avoid looking at themselves put the blame for their negativity on the "unconscious," as if it were an ugly black bucket of demons and evil that comes with them as part of their equipment at birth and over which they have no control or understanding.

Your mother and father, not horrible demons inside you, are the source of your emotional problems. And their parents before them were the source of their emotional problems. For negative love is *passed on* from generation to generation.

Some people have difficulty in recalling their childhood, as if the forgetfulness were so strong that it is irreversible. Nothing could be further from the truth. Anything that influenced us must have been in the awareness at some level and can be brought back to the awareness with the proper tools. We are not a prisoner of our unconscious. Everything we need to know to understand how and why we became the way we are is available for recall and re-examination if we learn how to do it. Fortunately, once in the awareness, negative love patterns can be dealt with and eliminated no matter how deeply they may have been buried. (How this is done is discussed in some detail in the second half of this book.)

At this point many books say, or imply, something like: "Now that you know why you're doing all those awful things to yourself, STOP. Now go and sin no more." With negative love it's not that simple. Admonitions and lip service are not the answers.

In the same way, you cannot just decide to be different than you have been conditioned to be. Breaking free of the negative love trap requires work on the emotional, intellectual, and spiritual levels. Since the intellect is like a speck on an ocean of emotion, simply reading about emotional negative love patterns only enables you to learn more about how you "ought" to be with yourself and others, without removing the negative love pattern itself. The result is only more conflict between intellectually based knowledge and the emotional resistance to change.

At the same time that a part of you is "trying" to get free, another part is fighting change with all the guile, strength, and resourcefulness it can muster. We have already seen it as the negative emotional child, which is the part of you that never got past age thirteen and is still negatively in love with Mommy and Daddy. While your intellect and body may have continued to grow, your emotional self still behaves as a child.

It is the negative emotional child that resists change and growth. Thus, people often go into therapies of one kind or another telling themselves they sincerely want to stop suffering and solve their problems. In fact, it is often their intellect that knows they would be happier if they solved their problems, while the child inside is content to remain negatively in love with the parents. At some point there comes a critical choice: being "true" to Mommy and Daddy or breaking free and risking the loss of their love. It is as if the person, secretly but fully comprehending what is really involved in change, says to himself, "If that's what it takes to get well, I think I'll stay sick. For a while longer anyway." The truth is getting a loving divorce from your parents brings autonomy and freedom as well as a positive new love relationship. A *loving* divorce is possible whether your parents are dead or alive.

Often people are not ready to put their lives together until they are down so low they have to reach up to touch bottom. Then they are usually ready to take responsibility for themselves and do something to change. Responsibility alone is not the full truth, for we did not make ourselves neurotic. We learned to be neurotic at our parents' misguidance and example. Therefore, to upbraid ourselves or others with being responsible for our problems is simply another admonition leading to further conflict and grief. Self-blame only adds to the misery while doing nothing to promote change or relief.

On the other hand, if you know what the problem is, and you have the tools and power to solve it, it does make good sense to free yourself. As you will see further on, life is beautiful without negative love. If you learned how to make yourself miserable, with the right help you can learn to make yourself happy. For whatever is learned can be unlearned.

Change *is* possible. The key word in the definition of negative love is *adopt*. When expressing negative love, the traits are yours only by adoption. In truth they are not yours; they are not inherently *you*. They are not hereditary or genetically based. There is nothing inevitable or fated in what you became in response to the emotional covert or overt blackmail by your parents. The growth of the emotional cancer, no matter how long it's been going on or how severe its consequences, is reversible. You learned how to be neurotic, and you can learn how to be free.

Do people really change through identifying and learning how to drop their negative love patterns? Here is a note from a young woman named Mary Ellen. At age thirty-three she had recently left the cloistered life of a nun. Although physically beautiful, she was frightened, lonely, brow-knitted, unhappy, irritable, frustrated, and paranoid. She was almost literally frightened of her own shadow.

> *I bought a secondhand wooden table, Bob, which proved to be a perfect physical, tangible expression of what we're doing on a psychological level. The table was such a mess on top. At first glance, it seemed almost unsalvageable. There were circles of ink penetrating the wood, burnt marks where hot objects had been unthinkingly placed, and deep cuts where people had ignorantly and carelessly used knives. The more I sanded, the more sympathy I began to have for this poor, defenseless piece of wood. It was so marred by carelessness and ignorance. When I got through the layers of dirt and the old finish, I could begin to see a really beautiful wood grain underneath. Interestingly enough, as I sanded it, I began to identify with the table. I was having a very bad time previously putting blame for my scarred, ugly, deficient self on everybody except me. It was true, I was not good enough. I simply deserved to be abandoned, like the table was by its previous owner. But as I sanded, I began to feel, by the very physical act of removing the scars, this poor, defenseless table really mirrored me as I had been in the past. And as the scars were removed—true with great effort and difficulty—I am sure that the table could feel, with great pain, my scars. I knew then that all the bad trips laid on me could also be removed. I now understand this. The table, now beautiful, with a brand-new finish, stands in my living room.*

What Mary Ellen discovered in this beautiful experience is that the world as she had known it was a lie. By removing the scars of the table, she was able to return it to its natural beauty of what it was. By removing the emotional cancer of lovelessness caused by the "virus" of negative love, she was able to return to the beauty of her basic positive essence—her spiritual self. Later the war between her intellect and her emotions ceased. In place of that conflict she was able to mature and become a Quadrinity, which is the term I use for the fully integrated four aspects of our selves: 1) intellect, 2) emotions, 3) spirit, and 4) physical body. Once negative love is dropped by the emotional child, the positive emotional child can grow up and be integrated into a whole, loving union with its present-day intellect, spirit, and body. This precious gift is available to everyone once they get a loving divorce from Mother and Dad.

CHAPTER III

"NOW WILL YOU LOVE ME?"

A book about love is incomplete without a discussion of one of its most powerful means of expression: *sex.* Often when I ask people, "How's your love life?" they think I mean, "How's your sex life?" Although closely related, the two are vastly different.

This brings us to another rude question. How *is* your sex life? Do you have the kind of sex you want as often as you like? Is sex a regular part of your life or something you only wish for? Is it varied enough to remain fresh and exciting for you? Or have you fallen into a familiar pattern that is comfortable but dull? Does the fulfillment meet your anticipation? Or are you usually left feeling empty and blue?

Beside your own pleasure, do you give sexual pleasure to your partner? Are you happy pleasing the other person? Do you give to give, or only give to get something in return? While thinking of your answers, bear in mind that in sex, as in love, it takes courage and honesty to face the truth.

How do you relate to your sex partner? Is it someone you value and care deeply about? Is it someone who values you and cares deeply for you? Or are you virtual strangers, using each other's bodies for a brief attempt to escape from boredom or loneliness?

Is your sexual relationship solely that, or do you also share other parts of your life with your partner? Is your sex partner part of your life before and after sex? Are you able to share tender, intimate moments together afterward as well as before and during sex? (If you have more than one sexual partner, answer the questions for each one.)

More importantly, how do you feel about your sexuality? How do you compare with your ideal for a person of your sex, age, and background? If you aren't expressing your sexuality the way you think you should, how far short are you falling?

You can get the most benefit from this book by taking a few moments to think about your answers. It is helpful to make notes of self-observations in order not to lose the clarity of your first thoughts. It is sometimes difficult, painful, or discouraging to see how we are really living our sex lives. Yet looking is the only way to confront the problems and learn what to do about them.

What about your parents? Look at their sex life in the same way. Did they have the kind of sexual life they wanted? Were they able to give pleasure to each other with a mixture of passion and tenderness? Was sex a regular, joyous part of their lives, or an obligation they reluctantly fulfilled out of duty to each other?

How did they feel about their own sexuality? Was your father secure in his masculinity, or did he constantly have to prove himself with conquests and affairs? Did he seek sexual fulfillment away from home? Was your mother secure in her femininity, or did she need constant reassurance that she was an attractive, sexual woman? Having been denied your father did she look elsewhere for sexual pleasure?

Some people may resist the suggestion that they look at their parents' sex life. Their rationale is "I never saw my parents doing it," or "This is prying into private matters." Actually having seen them in bed isn't necessary in order to understand their sex life together. Did they display love, affection, and warmth for each other? And for you? If they never touched you, it's likely they seldom touched each other. Were they able to joke about sex from time to time? Or was sex so filled with taboos and prohibitions that they couldn't laugh about it?

Look also at how they handled your sexual education. How did your parents teach you the facts of life? As you approached adolescence, did they discuss it comfortably with you? Were they able to give you clear, reliable information about the changes in your body as you became a physical adult? Were they able to deal compassionately and reassuringly with your questions and fears? Were they also able to share with you the joy of your joining them in adulthood? Were they able to give you the emotional maturity needed to prepare you for real adult sexuality? If you have a sexual problem right now, could you discuss it frankly with your mother and father?

Or did they avoid the subject and shirk their responsibility? Did they perhaps slip you a book and say, "Here, read this"? Did they leave it to some other adult, perhaps a doctor, schoolteacher, or religious counselor to assist you through this critical transition in your life?

Or did they do nothing at all, leaving you to fend for yourself, almost certain to pick up misinformation and superstitions from your equally uninformed friends?

Have you had difficulty rising above your parents' level of sexual knowledge? Could you easily and knowingly tell a twelve-year-old boy or girl the facts of sexual life without sniggering as if sex were dirty or stammering as if sex were frightening? Can you accurately describe the structure and function of the sexual and reproductive organs in man and woman? Could you tell a naive youngster what he or she needs to know about masturbation, birth control, and venereal disease? Could you tell a young man or woman how to enjoy sex without exploiting others? And can you back up your instruction with your own living example? Would you advise a young person to live his or her sexual life as you have lived yours? And would they be wise to follow your counsel? Or would you have to cop out and say, "Do as I say, not as I do?"

Yes, these are thought-provoking questions. Almost no one who answers honestly will be completely satisfied with what he sees in himself. People who have love problems usually have sexual problems. My point is that discomfort with sex proves that parents who had sexual difficulties continue as a negative influence in their childrens' lives today. If your mother and father did not have an adequate sexual adjustment coupled with feelings of love and tenderness for each other, they were unable to teach these qualities to you. Children of sexually confused, frightened, ignorant, defensive, or prudish parents are presented with two unsatisfactory choices. They can adopt mother's and father's basically unhealthy, immature sexual attitudes along with their awkwardness or ignorance about sex. Or they can rebel against mother's and father's example, attempting to be free of their influence while covering up the conflict that inevitably follows on the heels of such rebellion. Either way, the result is a stunted, incomplete sex life.

Nor are the children of "liberated" parents much better off. Where sex is treated as casually as if it were just another physical function like eating, drinking, or urinating, children are cheated of the opportunity to experience the spiritual and positive emotional side of sexual love. It is an error to assume that if mother and father had no sexual inhibitions, they therefore had no sexual problems. The inability to see beyond the physical side of sex to its emotional, spiritual, and intellectual dimensions is as much a problem as the common inability to fully enjoy the physical experience of sex.

After looking at mother's and father's sex life, compare it with your own. If you are living your sexual life differently than your parents did, either more permissively or more conservatively, is it easy for you? Are you really free of the example they set for you? Or do you have to struggle against pangs of guilt or anger for rebelling against them?

On the other hand, if your sex life is similar to theirs, are you happy with it? Would you change it if you could? How much would things have to change for you to be happy, however you define happiness?

Like the ability to love, the ability to enjoy adult sexuality without guilt or fear does not only depend on conditions "out there," such as your partner's ability to turn you on. Sexual pleasure also comes from your freedom and ability to turn yourself on. We learn, or more often don't learn, to enjoy a full sexual life by the example our parents set for us. Does this mean parents should invite their children into the bedroom with them? Of course not. Their sex life is and should be their private domain. Being sexually honest with children doesn't necessarily mean discussing your own sexual problems with them. Yet to give children adequate preparation for adult life, parents must acknowledge the existence of sexual life and prepare them for it with open positivity and love.

If you are among those who know how to love, you understand what I am saying. The sexual experience must reach beyond passion to include tenderness, variety, openness, and surrender. While sexual fulfillment is affected by whom you are with and what you are doing, the level you reach is ultimately up to you. This is when the body becomes alive, aware and open to its total sensitivity. Complete sex encompasses your entire self: the spiritual essence, the emotional goodness, and yes, the intellectual ability to understand and permit what's happening. When your quadrinity of body, spirit, emotions, and intellect, merge with the quadrinity of *your* partner, the experience of fulfillment is sheer ecstacy.

Most of us never reach the heights of sexual ecstasy on all *four* levels of being because of the fetters of negative love which keep us from experiencing sex as a total experience. Sexuality is controlled by negative love like any other area of life.

Whether a child becomes masculine or feminine, tough or tender, lusty or frustrated, hot or cold, promiscuous or celibate, is determined by the negative love programming inflicted on him during his childhood. The effect is the manner in which he expresses the programming during adulthood.

Sexual difficulties, however distressing they may be, are only symptoms of the deeper problem: the inability to love. It is necessary to explore the symptom and trace its cause. The remedy for sexual problems is the same as for all neurotic problems: *love* that nourishes the individual and enables him to share that emotional goodness with others. Love for self and others leads you easily and effortlessly toward growth and fulfillment, in sex as in every other aspect of life.

For a deeper understanding of sexual problems, let's look beneath the apparent diversity of sexual behavior to the motivating efforts behind the act. Instead of asking, "What are people doing sexually?" let's ask, "Why are people doing what they are doing?"

By asking "Why?" instead of "What?" we get not hundreds, or perhaps thousands, of categories of behavior, but only the two aspects of the negative love pattern: negative love or rebellion. When a child adopts the negative traits, moods, silent or spoken admonitions of his parents, he is expressing negative love for them. In rebellion, the child rejects mother and father and chooses from among the variety of contrary ways to engage in sex. Rebellion against negative love leads to conflict and frustration. Sexual rebellion leads to conflict because the programmed child within the adult is risking the loss of Mommy's and Daddy's love by disobeying them. ("Child within the adult" refers to the emotional part of us that is stuck in the past, still relating to the mother and father we knew during childhood.) When parents send mixed messages or set an inconsistent example, children become confused and frightened. As a result, most people experience sex with a combination of negative love and rebellion.

One of the more common sexual problems is boredom. Sex so often becomes more a duty than a pleasure. Women who are "supposed" to do it, rarely find an element of joy in the act. This form of "sexual blahs" is the often-voiced complaint of the housewife. It also extends to working women, married or single.

The sexual wasteland is created by parents who didn't enjoy sex and couldn't teach their children to enjoy it. Often mother was a drudge who worked so hard she had no time or energy left for joyful sex with her husband. The vibes in her house were dull and tense from fatigue and overwork. Father was perhaps aloof and undemonstrative, showing little affection for his wife or his children.

Sexually bored women are usually relating to mother and father with simple negative love. Mother was overworked, overfed, underpaid, and underloved, and daughter is living her own life the same way. "See, Mom and Dad?" her negative emotional child is saying. "Life's a drag just like you said. There was no time for fun, especially sex. I'm just like you. *Now* will you love me?"

Men, too, fall victim to similar programming: "Sex is no fun. Work hard and forget about it." In fact, people with this programming tend to marry each other and live out boring lives together. Like his wife, the husband in such a marriage expresses his negative love to his parents by marrying someone who is hard-working and non-sexual. His mother, like his wife, was so overworked and underappreciated that she had little time or energy to show any love or enthusiasm for her husband. Out of negative love to mother, he married a girl "just like the girl who married dear old Dad."

He got the admonition, "Wives aren't sexual. Settle down and forget sex." Which is what he does. His father, like his wife's father, was unimaginative, distant, undemonstrative, and usually not fully *there* for his wife and children. Through their negative love programming the two were unfortunately made for each other.

Both the husband and the wife in this situation would prefer to rebel and live the fuller lives they were truly made for, but they are so trapped in negative love that they cannot live differently without plunging themselves into deeper conflict and guilt. Most of the time their lives are not unbearable since their hard work is an energy outlet and provides money enough for more than necessities. They tend not to rock the boat or cause trouble, but below the surface they are leading "lives of quiet desperation."

The real problem for each of these people is not that they aren't getting enough sex. They certainly would feel better and have more fun if they were getting more sex, but *their real problem is no love.* Perhaps mother and father taught them to be polite and well-behaved, which is to say, phony. Their relationship with each other is flat and mechanical. They go through the motions of family life without experiencing the warmth of love that make the family more than a physical convenience or an economic advantage. Born out of love for each other, sex is not a duty; it's ecstatic sharing. Instead of dragging at the end of the day, he's eager to get home to her, and she's eager to greet him lovingly. They love to be together, for each is the other's best friend. When the tone is loving, each loves to be there for the other; bedtime becomes a joyous celebration of true love.

Boredom isn't the only way to adopt the negative love traits of mother and father. The wildest kind of compulsive, promiscuous sexing can also be an expression of negative love. "Like father, like son" applies to sex as to other areas. Often the man who chases every woman in sight, married or single, young or old, is imitating what he saw his father doing (or what his father wished *he* had done in his own youth). If his mother also had casual sexual affairs, a man's pattern of much sex with no emotional involvement will be a double negative love adoption of both parental traits. His father's admonition may have been, "Women are there for the taking, but don't get trapped." And mother's silent or overt admonition is often complementary, "Women are for sex but not love."

"See, Mom and Dad?" says the negative emotional child within, "I'm having lots of sex just the way you did. But I'm not letting anyone fulfill me any more than you did, so I'm not outdoing you. I'm still your little boy. *Now* will you love me?"

To avoid outdoing mother and father, the compulsive sexer, male or female, will usually run from anyone who appears to offer real emotional involvement or asks for real emotional commitment. In adopting negative love traits, the slogan, no matter what the behavior, reflects the idea from one of the old gospel songs: "It was good for my mother; it was good for my father; and it's good enough for me."

People with compulsive sexual appetites rarely get more than a temporary superficial pleasure. When sex is only physical, there is always something missing. Men and women with no experience of the nonphysical dimensions of sex may know that something is missing without being able to identify it. They search for years for the ultimate sexual experience that will make it happen. It never does because what they seek is always lacking the positive emotional and spiritual components of sex. Out of negative love to mother and father they remain one-dimensional beings never attaining the ultimate.

Adopting an admonition from mother or father doesn't necessarily mean becoming like them, as the following story illustrates. Charles was a fragile, effeminate boy, a great disappointment to his masculine, heterosexual father. His father tried without success to coax, cajole, or threaten his son into behaving like the typical rough-and-tumble boy. Instead, Charles was an indoor type who did well in school, which only heightened his father's frustration since he himself had been a poor student.

Although Charles, feeling non-accepted, rebelled against his father's masculine traits, he adopted a deeper, more powerful admonition: "You are a pansy. Get away from me." In reply his negative emotional child said: "O.K., Dad, whatever you say. I am a pansy. *Now* will you love me?" Charles never lost his deep longing for his father's love, so he sought it in this illogical way. Each person's negative love syndrome is a mixture of adoption and rebellion. Charles showed both, but his dominant theme was adopting the admonition, "You are a pansy."

When he left home, he moved to a large city, joined the gay community, and lived like the "pansy" his father said he was. He was attracted to masculine men who resembled his father. Charles sought from them the male approval and acceptance he desperately needed and had missed.

He also expressed negative love for his mother through his homosexuality. She felt guilty for producing a "queer" son and for not really wanting him. To assuage her guilt, she overreacted, smothering him with attention and protection, especially when her husband would berate the boy for his lack of manliness. After each brutal tongue-lashing, Charles would run to her and buy his face in her bosom while she stroked his hair and soothed his crushed ego. "There, there," she would purr. "It's all right. Mother understands. Sit here while I dress, and we'll go for a walk together." Boys learn to be masculine by emulating their father's masculinity. Charles continued to stay close to his mother since she was the only source of any kind warmth for him. While remaining close to his mother, he grew more and more distant from his father. As an adult, when he dressed in female clothes, he was indeed emulating mother.

Obviously, not all male homosexuals had rejecting fathers and smothering, overprotective mothers. Homosexuality, like any other sexual orientation or preference, has *myriad* potential sources, far too many to cover completely in this small volume. Some men who got along very well with father had mothers who were cold and distant. They adopted the silent admonition, "Women are unloving." In adulthood we create our own emotional world based on what we were taught to expect. For a boy with a warm father and cold mother, his adult world may contain warm men as friends and lovers and reject women. Here, too, the negative emotional child is saying, "You were right, Mom and Dad. A man's best friend is another man."

Homosexuals, both male and female, are not sick, any more than are their heterosexual brothers and sisters. Most are caught up in negative love patterns that determine how their inherent sexuality is expressed, and most need to learn how to love themselves and others on all four levels of their being. With self-love, homosexuals can also have healthy, loving relationships.

Parents also teach their children to be afraid of sex. Often a frigid woman had a mother who taught her that sex was dirty and disgusting. Out of straight negative love to mother, the girl will adopt mother's trait. In adult life she may avoid sex completely by never having any male friends. Even if she marries, she will often avoid sex by choosing a male as unsexual as she is.

Father is the source of many of a woman's sexual fears. One morning as she was getting out of bed, little Alice heard her father whistling as he shaved in the bathroom. Tiptoeing behind him, she saw that he was naked. He was absorbed in his morning ritual and didn't hear the barefoot child. Silently as she eased her head around his leg, she observed his penis hanging limp between his thighs.

Never having seen a penis, she said, "Daddy, what's that?"

Startled, embarrassed, and flustered, he replied angrily, "None of your business! Get out of here, go to your room."

"But, Daddy . . . " she stammered, "I . . . I . . . "

"Never mind," he barked as he quickly reached for a towel to wrap around his waist. "Get out of here! And don't ever come in here again without knocking."

Crushed, little Alice slunk away, vowing never again to be curious about that thing between Daddy's legs. As she grew older, she learned that it was a penis and that it had something to do with sex. But her powerful negative love admonition was, "Don't be curious about a man's penis, or he'll get angry and yell and resent you." To our adult intellect this may seem illogical or absurd, but to a four-year-old—and to the negative emotional child within an adult like Alice—it makes good sense. Whether she can remember it or not, every woman who fears sexual intercourse experiences variations of just such traumatic childhood experiences.

No matter how much time passes, or even how patient and understanding their husbands or lovers might be, women whose fathers or mothers frightened them and disapproved of their sexual curiosity are often doomed to live troubled sex lives until they are free to stop living out the negative love admonitions they heard as little girls.

The impotent man, like the frigid woman, is the product of his parents' teaching. While what they tell him may not be clearly about sex, it can nonetheless have a powerful sexual impact. As a young boy, for example, the impotent man may have heard his father violently and repeatedly flail him with

the taunt, "You're an idiot! You can't do *anything* right."
Since disobeying his father means risking the loss of his love,
the boy will often adopt the admonition that he can't do
anything right, *including sex.* Later in life, when his opportunity with a willing woman arrives, his negative love for
father may keep him from rising to the occasion.

Or his mother may have taught him to fear rejection by
being alternately warm and cold toward him. On a seesaw
of love, he never learned whether he deserved love or not.
He got just enough taste of a woman's love to want more,
but he's afraid to go all the way, in love or in sex, for fear the
woman will coldly reject him the way mother often did.

Since he fears that whatever he does won't be good
enough, this type often chooses not to risk failure and rejection, and after perhaps a few youthful attempts, avoids sex.
The tragedy is that often these men have normal sexual appetites, but their fear of failure keeps them from taking risks.
That old crippling message from mother and father, "You're
not good enough to please me," makes it impossible for the
man to take his place among sexually mature individuals.
Instead, he will remain his parents' incompetent little boy as
long as he continued to say, "OK, Mom and Dad. I'm the
bungler you always said I was. *Now* will you love me?"

The value of sex therapy is often limited. While frigid
women and impotent men can be taught how to make intercourse possible, the level of sexual fulfillment is limited by
the continuing effects of the negative love programming that
says, in effect, "Sex is a no no," and "You'll never make it."
This problem of competing parental messages is particularly
painful even in this day of sexual freedom. We hear messages
that say, "Go ahead! Break free. Do it, whatever turns you
on." Breaking free can mean almost anything; having sex
without marriage; using birth control; taking an extramarital
lover; having an abortion; experiencing homosexuality, or
one-night stands with strangers. I believe in freedom and have
dedicated my life to helping others find it. But it's impossible
to skip and jump through the fields of sexual bliss with the
ball and chain of negative love around your ankle. Breaking
free means disobeying the admonition, "Don't be freer than
Mommy and Daddy or we won't love you." What sexually
unfree men and women struggle against is not the social rules
of the time in which they live but the spoken or implied con-

fining sexual messages they received when they were children.

The real negative love programming is usually below the level of awareness, and people cannot be ordered, coaxed, or persuaded out of it. Attempting to do so merely causes more conflict and tension.

Linda came from a family in which love was just a word. Her mother was cold and aloof toward the occasional sexual advances of her father. His outlet was in work, sports, and an occasional "night on the town with the boys." With no physical touching from either parent, she grew up desperately longing for warmth of any kind. Although her parents didn't teach her to be sexual, she was a pretty girl with basic desires, and boys were attracted to her. Soon after her fourteenth birthday she had her first sexual experience. Although at first awkward and fumbling, she quickly learned that boys, and later men, would give her the warmth and approval she never got at home. Her parents attempted to stop what they called "her decline into wantonness and sin," but once she had a taste of warmth and approval, she couldn't get enough. When she ran away at seventeen, her emotional child said to her parents, "The hell with you. I'm going where I can have some fun and get some love. I'll show you." And so she did, gaining a reputation wherever she went as a warm, sexually free woman. Beneath her sexually free exterior, however, she was in terrible conflict over her rebellion. The more she tried, and failed, to get Daddy's love from her many sex partners, the more frustrated and empty she became. She couldn't give up sex because it felt good, and it was her ticket to popularity, nor could she really find fulfillment on a deep level because it was counter to mother's and father's admonition, "Don't be sexy. Don't touch people." Her tragedy, like that of many beautiful women who appear so loving, is that behind the facade lies desperate emptiness, loneliness, and conflict.

Almost any behavior contrary to the parents' sexual traits and admonitions will "work" as a form of rebellion because it is often indulged in not for its own sake but to get even with unloving mother and father. Women from families in which little love is shown, or in which sex is high and loose, may rebel in a socially acceptable way by withdrawing from the world of adult sex, preferring to be celibate. Rebellion need not be unconventional or unpopular to be effective. It only needs to go counter to what mother and father said and did.

Rebellion stemming from sibling rivalry usually has its sexual aspects as well. When a little girl feels displaced by her younger sister, for example, she may decide that no more positive attention is available and settle for her parents' negative attention. In conventional middle-class families this often is illustrated when the goody-goody younger sister compliantly marries a professional man and moves to the suburbs to raise well-behaved children. Her displaced older sister angrily rebels by not marrying and instead goes through a series of brief, superficial affairs that leave her feeling empty and exploited but "free of her parents' bourgeois morality."

When she does marry, the middle-class rebel often chooses the type of man her parents have the least regard for: perhaps a starving artist or a bohemian. Often she may work to support him which serves to further outrage her parents' rigid sense of propriety. While she genuinely suffers from the physical and financial deprivations of the "free" life, her inner emotional child gleefully watches her parents' distress. "I showed them. They wouldn't love me, so I ran away, and now they're sorry, aren't they? Look at me. Aren't I free?" The tragedy of such people is that their intellect knows they might be happier doing things differently from their parents, yet their emotions deny them the pleasure of real freedom.

The negative love pattern is no different with brothers. If one brother, either younger or older, gets all the positive attention, the other will often rebel, deciding that opposing mother and father is the way to get their negative attention. The bizarre, often destructive sexual lives of many single persons, either divorced or never married, are proof not of their freedom but of their angry childhood desire to rebel against mother and father. "See, Mommy and Daddy. Since you won't love me, I won't do what you want me to do. I'll get into trouble, and you'll be sorry. *Then* maybe you'll notice me."

Sexual rebellion can also be delayed until the middle years or later. The escapades of men and women in their forties and fifties are often the result of the years they compliantly bought mother's and father's pseudo-love by being "good," while receiving no genuine love in return. As they approach the middle of life and their parents begin to die off, the desire to make up for lost time takes hold. "The hell with it. I'm going to have some fun while there is still time." Such rebellions are fraught with painful conflict and usually end in failure. Rebellion never leads to love.

The reality of sexual life is often more complicated when a child receives mixed or contradictory sexual messages from his parents. When mother and father don't agree on sex, their children are left confused, frightened, and bitter as they flip-flop between pleasing father and pleasing mother.

Michael's story is typical of the child with such inconsistent parents. His father, a macho type, taught him that sex was OK, but that only sissies showed their feelings. His mother, a meek, clinging woman, was frightened of sex and never discussed it but showed him it was OK to feel hurt or frightened. Michael's deep sexual conflict was inevitable. With a father whose message was "Do it like a man," and a mother who said, "Sex is dirty," he was wrong no matter what he did. Obeying father, he compulsively chased women he had no feelings for while his negative emotional child asked, "How am I doing, Dad?" He had sex out of negative love to father but felt guilty over his rebellion against mother. At other times he obeyed mother and went long periods without sex while feeling depressed and lonely, which was rebellion against father. Feeling ambivalent, he was guilty in his relation to mother when he was having sex and unmanly in relation to father when he wasn't. Michael was ripped apart by his conflict until he learned how to free himself from his self-destructive negative love patterns.

Ruth's parents were more closely attuned in their sexual messages. She nonetheless found herself in a double-bind conflict. Her father thought casual sex was OK for men, telling her older brother, "Find 'em, feel 'em, fuck 'em, forget 'em." Since children often adopt messages meant for a sibling, she adopted this one as her own. Her mother thought sex was OK, but not before marriage. "Nice girls don't do it except with their husbands" was the way Ruth's mother put it.

As she grew to adulthood, Ruth felt bad no matter what she did. She didn't stop wanting the casual sex father advocated merely because mother told her to wait until the wedding. And she didn't stop hearing mother's forbidding voice in her head every time she had sex. When Mommy says, "No!" and Daddy says, "Go!" the emotional result can be pure hell: you can't win but to lose.

The man or woman who lives two sexual lives, one public, the other private, also responds to his conventional parents with both negative love and rebellion. A closet homosexual with a wife and children frustratingly lives in this split pattern. Out of negative love he outwardly leads a conventional, straight life. When he occasionally rebels, he finds a male partner and lives out his sexual fantasies. At the height of his orgasm with another man his negative emotional child may be riding high: "Whoopee! Fun, fun, fun." Later, he may be overwhelmed with guilt and remorse: "Gee, I'm sorry, Daddy. I couldn't help myself. If I feel bad enough about it, will you forgive me and love me?" His intellect may not hear the conversation, but his emotions sense the roar of conflict.

Negative love patterns are even more obvious in the extremes of sexuality, such as violence or total deprivation. If Daddy was a sadist who beat up mother before having sex with her, the child learns that screams and bruises are the proper kind of sexual foreplay. Many sadists and masochists cannot be sexually aroused in any other way, completely because of their negative love programming. When they are relieved of their unfortunate emotional attachment to their destructive parents, they can respond sexually as if they had never heard of the Marquis de Sade.

Women of sadistic tendencies are not necessarily imitating mother. Daddy is more often the culprit here. If he was cold or rarely home, she may be getting even with him by mistreating her masochistic husband or boyfriend. (The daughters of cold men get even in more places than in bed, in case you haven't been in divorce court or a shopping center lately.)

The nymphomaniac, too, suffers from a severe lack of father's love, often through death or abandonment. So deprived was she that no man can satisfy her, in bed or out, though she searches desperately from one bed to another for one who will. Even while she runs to a new sex alliance, her emotional child is saying, "It's OK, Daddy. I won't let anyone fulfill me any more than you did. I'll always be yours no matter who may try to take your place."

The rapist is dying of longing for mother's love. Perhaps it happened that when he cried in the night as an infant, mother ignored him and turned the music up. He could only get her attention by crying still louder. As he grew older he became even more demanding. He had to *take* what she wouldn't freely give him. When he rapes a resisting, terrified woman, he's in effect still taking from his unloving, resisting mother and getting even with her for the heartless, rejecting way she treated him as a child. His guilt and conflict stem from the pain of his negative emotional child, who gets "love" in this way. (This is only one of many causes of rape, but a primal one.)

There are many variations in the kinds of negative love programming leading to sexual deviance. We cannot cover them all here, but sex deviants in general are people who were pathetically deprived of love during childhood. The child molester, the voyeur, the fetishist, were all absolutely love starved and unfulfilled. The child molester is often reliving the relationship with a younger sister or brother. Depending on whether he's violent or harmless, he's either getting even with the rival who displaced him, or trying to prove that he really loved the rival whom he may have bullied and abused in childhood. In some cases the child molester painfully observed his mother give her love to a neighbor's child while ignoring him. In turning his adult sexual attention toward a child, he is acting out of negative love and rebellion. He adopts mother's trait by appearing to love the little girl or little boy. ("See, Mother, I'm loving a small child just the way you did. Now will you love me?") At the same time, his abuse of the child is a way of getting even with mother for not giving him the love he so desperately wanted. Of course, he is also getting even with the object of mother's affection.

The fetishist may have an amazing variety of peculiar sexual turn-ons. Whether his lust is for feet, underwear, shoes, vegetables, or the living room furniture, he takes the thing as a substitute for his childhood love: mother. Anything strongly linked with her in his mind will act as a trigger for his childhood longing. The voyeur, or Peeping Tom, suffers from an unsatisfied sexual curiosity. If mother made too big a fuss when he caught an accidental look at her while she was undressed, he may develop an overpowering desire to find out what the great secret is.

The spectrum of negative love and sex is much wider and more complex than one chapter can encompass. These few examples were given to shed some light on common sexual problems and how negative love programming is the villainous cause. No matter what the sexual problem, the answer is the same—love, enough to fill the void left by the parents who, for whatever reason, were not there in the way they were needed most: loving and accepting.

CHAPTER IV

MIND REVELATIONS

Since negative love to mother and father is *the* problem facing us, what is the solution? What can we do about it?

The answer is, was, and always will be the same: "the flowing, the rendering, the outgoing of the heart and soul of emotional goodness, to yourself first, then to those around you." The antidote to the poison of negative love is the power of *positive* love, experienced totally within oneself. After cleaning your diamond (spiritual self) it can then radiate unimpeded to others.

The important question is . . . How? How can you teach someone to love; to overcome years, perhaps an entire lifetime, of negative feelings and behavior? How can we rise above the muck and mire of negative love to the heights of positive love?

The way out is the same as the way in: programming. The negative love syndrome is a destructive form of mind programming. Mother's and father's negative traits, and the rebellion against them, are not genetic. They are adopted and can be unadopted. Learned misinformation *can* be unlearned. Not loving yourself and others is like any bad habit. You can learn to love by demolishing the negative love programming and replacing it with positive programming that frees you to be your true self.

The Quadrinity Process* teaches true love in exactly this way. First we learn how negative patterns that plague and distress us arise from the negative love programs we received from our parents during childhood. Greater awareness alone, however, is not enough. Secondly, the Process provides the tools that break up the programming that keeps us from experiencing loving spontaneity and autonomy.

To some, the Process description of how to teach love may seem pat and simple. Yet are not the most powerful truths often the most simple? Since to love or not to love is a matter of one's childhood training, then it must follow that love can be learned through a process of retraining.

First premises first. We are both physical and non-physical beings. The physical aspect is our body. It includes the brain, which is the organic structure that makes mental activity possible. The non-physical aspect has three parts: (1) the spirit, (2) the intellect, and (3) the emotions. Taken together, these three comprise the non-physical psychosoul spirit of Mind Trinity.

While we believe the spiritual self is a crucial aspect of each person, learning self-love does not depend on one's belief in spirituality or God. As one student said, "I didn't believe in the psychic stuff before I took the Process, and I don't *totally* believe it now, yet the Process works."

The negative love programming is recorded in our emotions during childhood. It also affects our intellect and obscures our perfect spiritual self. The push and pull of conflict we experience stems from the lack of integration between the present-day intellect and childhood emotions. The specific goal of reprogramming is to re-educate the emotional child within to drop its negative programming, grow up, and join its spiritual self and intellectual self in present-day harmony. When this newly mature Trinity merges with the physical self and becomes a total Quadrinity, the individual is free to act, think, feel, and most of all, to love as one with no conflict or inhibition. After being relieved of the negative love programming that keeps you fragmented, there is no more question of which part of you is running your life. There's just you, acting, feeling, thinking, and *being* love.

---

*See Afterword for information on the teaching of the Quadrinity Process.

Lack of integration in the Quadrinity is so common that most people mistakenly assume the split is natural. It is not! The integrated Quadrinity of body, spirit, intellect, and emotions is the way we were meant to be.

The programming from childhood, both positive and negative, is recorded in our minds much like information is recorded on a computer card. When the "computer card mind" is "inserted" into the physical brain, we behave according to the programming. Our brain does what our mind orders it to do. To experience how your mind programs your brain, gently close your eyes and in your mind's eye see yourself in a supermarket . . . (As you read, pause at the dots to visualize the scene fully.) Walk over to the fresh produce section . . . Note a large bin of beautiful, thick-skinned navel oranges. The orange aroma is strong. Select one. Mentally hold it in your hands and feel the pores of the skin . . . Smell it . . . Dig your fingers into the skin and peel it easily . . . Segment it and plop a juicy morsel into your mouth . . . Experience the orange juices on your taste buds, and swallow . . . Taste the orange sweetness . . . Fine! Now mentally walk to a counter of lemons and select a large, yellow lemon . . . Smell its lemony aroma . . . Nearby there's a cutting board and a knife. Place the lemon on the cutting board and slice it in two . . . Put half the lemon in your mouth and suck on it . . . Are you experiencing your mouth pucker? Are you salivating? Your physical reaction to the orange and lemon mind revelation demonstrates how the mind can be used to cause physiological activity. The Quadrinity Process mind revelations reprogram negative love to positive love. No, it's not brainwashing; it's mind cleaning. What you experienced is an example of a mind revelation. Far more sophisticated ones are used in our work to remove blocks to loving.

There are two kinds of mental pictures, similar in appearance but different in origin. With our active imagination, which is under our control, we use our conscious minds intentionally to create an image. This is projective visualization.

Receptive visualization, on the other hand, is what we allow to enter our mind without forcing, trying or projecting. Receptive visualizing often occurs while we are daydreaming or "staring off into space." Dreams are another form of receptive, as opposed to projective, "seeing." The images are simply there, without our consciously summoning or directing them.

The ability to receive and see mental images originating outside ourselves is part of everyone's natural sensory perception (NSP). This ability is within each of us, waiting to be developed. Everyone can learn to see with the inner eye (in psychic terms known as clairvoyance) and hear with the inner ear (clairaudience). As with any other natural ability, some people have more potential than others, but everyone *can see* and *hear* psychically after some basic instruction and a brief period of practice. (ESP is a misnomer. It's not *Extra*, it's *Natural.*)

The importance of NSP in the Process is that it gives clients a wide range of tools for reprogramming. Long-buried memories are easily recalled.

The following excerpt is taken from the Process notes of a man who discovered the difference between mental projection and mental reception NSP.

> *You assigned us a mind revelation in class. We were to see ourselves in our bedroom and visualize the closest person to us entering who would call us by name and say something pleasant to us. In doing it, I tried to see my wife, but no go. I tried to see several others. Then all of a sudden my thirteen-year-old daughter appeared and said, "Daddy, I love you." I was surprised to find that my intended imagined projection of my wife didn't work in this mind realm. Instead of my wife, my daughter entered. Surprise! I now see that the mind revelations are not projected imagery.*

With this brief preparation and understanding you are now ready to experience an adventurous mind revelation. You will experience a mental place of peace, your personal sanctuary, and meet a loving spiritual guide and teacher. It would help if someone would read the following to you or you could record it and then play it back.

To help you relax, sit well back in your chair, gently close your eyes, take in a deep breath with the soft sound of "i" as in "in," and exhale through your mouth with a long sound of *sch* (like letting air out of a balloon). I . . . Sch . . . Do this three times. When you feel yourself quite relaxed, proceed.

Send your non-physical self (your Trinity) or mind out

into space where there is total nothingness. See absolutely nothing . . . Now in front of you permit a large, rectangular white screen to appear. Let the screen descend slowly . . . As the screen descends, you will see first a blue sky, then a tranquil refuge, a place that gives you a feeling of comfort and peace, perhaps a woodland meadow, a beach, or a mountain setting. Note the trees, flowers, grass, and other details of this lovely natural setting. This is your sanctuary.

Take a leisurely walk along the pathways. Experience the wonderful feeling of belonging. Feel the warmth of the sun caressing you. Listen to the song of the birds. You have found your mind's home, a place to refresh your soul and find succor.

As you walk along a path, you see in the distance a luminous white glow. It appears to be a circular light. Stop about five feet in front of it. Let it slowly descend. You will sense there is someone standing behind the light. Look first to see the hair. Note the color and style. Then, as the light continues to descend, note the shape of the forehead. Then a pair of beautiful, loving eyes appear. As the disc descends further, there are the cheekbones and nose. Then the lips and the chin. The entire loving face is now visible.

The disc continues to descend, revealing the neck, shoulders, and torso. Note the mode of dress. There before you is your guide. Walk up to your guide as if removing a mask. A true guide will not object. If the face comes off, you have encountered an impostor. Mentally tell the impostor to leave your sanctuary, continue walking along the path, and repeat the descending disc process as many times as necessary until you get a guide who *cannot* be unmasked.

When you have your real guide, ask his or her name. The first thought impression will be your guide's name. Accept what you hear or see.

Raise your hands, touch your fingertips to your guide's, and send energy to him or her. Speak to your guide mentally, saying, "Carve out thousands of acres of this lovely parkland as our private sanctuary, and build a stone wall around it so high and so thick that no one can enter." You are now in a protected fortress sanctuary with your guide. Ask your guide to take you to the wall and blast a tunnel through it. Now have him or her erect solid bronze doors every ten feet down the length of the tunnel. You hold the master key to these doors. Give the key to your guide, saying, "As my spiritual guide and guardian, I trust you to protect me from all negative forces." Your guide then opens all the doors with the master key. Ask your guide to cleanse your sanctuary of all mental forces, both positive and negative, so that the sanctuary will be totally yours. He or she searches everywhere in the sanctuary and ushers out all such psychic forces. The positive ones leave willingly, knowing there are other places for them in the endless universe. The negative forces don't want to leave. So your guide uses his or her power, along with your added energy and forcibly ejects all the negative forces from your sanctuary. They cannot withstand your combined strength and are drawn from the mountain, valleys, rivers, streams, lakes, beaches, and fields toward the doors. They fly past you and down the tunnel as if drawn by a giant vacuum machine attached to the outermost door of your sanctuary tunnel. Your guide then makes a last check of the sanctuary to be sure they are all out. He or she finds a last holdout, perhaps behind a boulder. This most negative and resistant of all forces grips tenaciously to the boulder, but your guide's hypnotic gaze and power pries it loose and sends it plummeting down the tunnel out of your sanctuary.

As you and your guide stand at the tunnel door, he or she gently turns to you and asks you to disrobe. Your guide then peels off all old encrusted negativities from your psychic mind body. This is the negative crud that has blighted you from the *psychic* side of life. As your guide removes the negativities, he or she tosses them down the tunnel. Your guide then looks deep within you, as if you were transparent, removes any lingering negative forms buried hidden within you, sends them out the tunnel, and then locks the door. Your guide holds his or her hands over your center and sends forth a healing light to balm and soothe. Allow yourself to experience this.

Your guide then takes you to a lovely watering place. The water is inviting. Plunge in. Delight yourself with the refreshing sensation of the cleansing water. Romp and splash with happy abandonment. After playing ease onto your back and float. Lazily you let yourself drift and feel the sun caressing you. Later, feeling refreshed, lift yourself onto the shore. Your guide gently towels you dry and gives you a garment similar to his or hers. You feel wonderful as you and your guide walk to a shaded and flowered glen and sit beneath a tree.

As you sit side by side, talk to your guide as you would to an old, trusted friend. Ask your guide a question. The answer will be given. Take paper and pencil in hand and record the conversation. You have found your guide and sanctuary and may return as often as you like, especially when you need a moment's peace and relaxation. Each time you do this your guide will give you the love, guidance and support you need to continue your journey. By the way, true guides are also never sex objects.

If you have had trouble or encountered anything frightening or negative in this mind revelation, it is *vital* for protective purposes to use the mind revelation that follows. Again close your eyes, do three long *isches*, relax and send your Trinity into the empty space. Let the space become an all-consuming white blinding light which obliterates all that is behind it. After the light disintegrates, all will be emptiness again. When you open your eyes, the negative experience will be out of your mind and never cause you distress.

People have various experiences finding their guide and sanctuary. For some it's easy; others have difficulty. At first you may doubt the validity of your perceptions, which is understandable since this is an unfamiliar mode of consciousness for most. Try not to judge what you see. With the proper help and patience everyone succeeds at it and finds much needed comfort. The following examples are a few typical experiences. Janice begins by describing her sanctuary.

> *It's a vast meadow, brilliantly alive with wild flowers of the most vivid kind—especially California poppies, in bright orange, and the blues of small cornflowers. There are also myriad tiny white flowers on the meadow. It stretches almost limitlessly and is sheltered by huge Alpine mountains; they have some trees on them, but above the timberline they are rather a deep maroon color, towering majestically, but not forbidding. I am surprised by the sense of light and the smell of the air. The light is warm and alive, the sky is a brilliant intense blue, the temperature is balmy but somehow brisk,*

*and the air has an invigorating quality to it. A kind
of electric joy emanates from the place. It is brilliantly but peacefully alive—open yet sheltered.*

*A brilliant disc of light appears, and gradually a
form begins to appear. Hair first—dark black, coiled
in a heavy top knot; a large and serene forehead,
shapely brows, and the most limpid amber-colored
(brown-yellow) eyes I have ever seen. They look
like eyes that understand suffering and have compassion. They seem somewhat sad. Very delicate
features—a straight nose and rounded chin, slender
neck held regally erect. The rest of the body mater-
ializes. I see her as a Hindu Indian woman whose
limbs are supple, with lovely, shapely hands, and
long, unpolished nails. She is tall, perhaps a little
taller than I, regal, and rounded without being at
all plump. She has a beautiful, shapely bosom
draped in the folds of her sari, which is of gauzy
stuff, deep green with rosy-red border. She has
golden sandals on her feet.*

*We touch each other's hands, and she smiles,
transforming that slightly pensive air to radiance.
Her name is Lokani. I feel that she is slightly older
than I, enough, say, to have been an older sister;
not old enough to be my mother. I don't feel at all
jealous or competitive with her, even though she is
far more beautiful and graceful than I. She loves
me and protects me. She wishes no harm to me.
She leads me to a pool made by a stream. We undress and bathe in the pool together. Although it is
sun-dappled and partly in the shade, the water is
warm and smells of pine and balsam, and we sport
in the pool like children. I am delightfully surprised
by her playfulness. It is as if suddenly we were
both much younger, and I am the playful loving
child I was never allowed to be, laughing and playing tag, dashing into the water. Although we are
both nude and admire each other's bodies, there is
nothing sexual in this context. Lokani hands me a
towel and dries my back. She dresses and hands me
a sari much like hers except it is deep blue (a color
I like) with a rosy border, and we walk off back*

to the fields again, touching hands occasionally.

We talk very little. She calls me Janice but says, "Sometimes I will call you the name I have given you: Jatma. That will be special for when we meet here." She smiles and shows brilliantly white teeth. Her English is beautiful and cultivated, with only the slightest trace of Indian accent. She has been educated abroad. I don't know yet much about who she was or what she did, but I know instinctively she is very wise, that she is especially wise about men, that she has great dignity and serenity, and yet withal, this surprising sense of play. She can go from being a kind of woodsprite to being a queen without any disjunction or confusion. She embodies all these things, so she is always herself in whatever face she presents.

When I tried to pull off her face, she at first reached a hand up as if to defend herself and then took it away to permit me to test her if I must. But I got the sense that my pulling at her face hurt—it was a real face.

Her inability to pull off the guide's face proves that Janice had met her real guide. Had the face been a mask, the guide would have been an impostor. If you get an impostor, it is important to send it away emphatically. There must be no doubt that your sanctuary is completely free of negative forces and totally controlled by you and the nurturing spirit of your *true* guide.

Some people find false guides that are projections of their current concerns or problems. Your real guide is never someone you know or a famous person. Often negative spirits masquerade as Jesus, Buddha or other religious teachers.

Above all, your guide is supportive and nurturing in a wise, loving way. Betty entered the Process with many problems, among them a great deal of self-consciousness and embarrassment about her appearance. She wrote:

My guide was a man and very fair, with a kind of light radiating out from his body all around. He seemed all golden and white . . . robed in white with the gold aura about it. His name is Roan or

Rowen. I know I can trust him and that he is all for me and only for good. Here is a dialogue I had with him.

Roan: *Here in the sanctuary everything that you will and wish with your heart and intellect can come to pass. I can see you as the beautiful soul you are. The negativity falls away under my gaze, and to me you are perfect.*

Betty: *That is hard for me to imagine, that you see through the crap as if it wasn't there. It is all too much to me. It feels like I am carrying around excess weight. And you don't think my negativities are my fault and that I'm inadequate and hopeless?*

Roan: *(Laughs with the sound of wind chimes) Stop that! You can trust my love, and you can trust that whom I love is really there. The radiance that is you, I can see and you will learn to see, too. Just wait and it will all come clear to you. I am here to help you reach that perfect point and then to stay there in clear focus.*

Betty's guide's reassurance helped to strengthen the positive within her.

Head trippers at first sometimes have difficulty seeing with their inner eye and getting the guide. Once they learn to tune out their intellects temporarily and allow other dimensions of their mental abilities to come through, the results are surprising. "It was hard to see the guide at first," wrote Al.

Hair and forehead would not jell behind the white disc. They kept changing from a woman's forehead with long brown hair to a man's with strong brow and "butch" haircut. Finally resolved into another naked woman, but with features: taut cheeks, narrow eyes, long face—tense and tough looking. I did not like or trust her, so pulled the face away. Very difficult.

Finally it came off, and there was my friend Marcel, a man. That would not do. I had to pull again. After much searching, my guide turned out to be an old Jewish rabbi, some long-dead ancestor from the seventeenth century named Zev. He seemed incongruous in my Alpine meadow, in his black caftan and black hat. I did not like or trust him instantly, but after a moment I began to feel his solidity. His face was amorphous, somewhat variable. We touched hands, embraced. That helped. He was silent.

The next day Al added this postscript to his guide and sanctuary dialogue.

Al: *You mean this crap that Bob's talking about really is real?*

Zev: *It is possible through these doors to move toward harmony not only within myself but with nature/vibrations/God/spirit. The experience comes and goes, but when it is with me, it is an incredibly vivid, strong, and personally real vision of how things can be.*

The element of surprise is often a good sign in the guide and sanctuary mind revelation. It shows that you didn't invent or create what you are seeing, which is exactly the point of Al's notes. You cannot create your guide; you can only be receptive to who and what is there. Here is how a student, Robert, learned this for himself.

My interest, so far, is to let the mind revelations flow. My guide is someone named Joseph. He has mixed gray-black-white hair, scraggly, reaching a little below his shoulders. As the disc was descending in front of my guide, I was hoping for a beautiful, warm woman, but this man with his head tilted slightly down appeared. Even though I tried to change him, or replace him with a woman, he steadfastly, stoically, lovingly remained in space and wouldn't budge.

A dialogue can be just like a person-to-person conversation.

Guide: *Since you believe in me, why don't you like the way I look? Why do you fight this image of me?*

Natalie: *I guess you look a little like a "jock"—those mindless pretty athletes. I've never had much in common with them. And you're blond! I don't usually respond to blonds. I can't really feel they have an intellect.*

Guide: *Ah, the old intellect game. You still want the intellect in the old sense—even though you really do know how limited that is. There's knowing and there's KNOWING. Don't concern yourself with mind games. The real KNOWING doesn't need those explanations.*

Natalie: *OK. Level with me. Who's **really** talking now, you or me?*

Guide: *You know. (He smiles.)*

Whatever you see and hear, do not be in awe of your guide. He or she is there to help you. The guide is like a wise, loving friend with whom you can take a peaceful stroll through your beautiful sanctuary whenever you need a release from stress or the answer to a problem. The guide also serves as a model as you learn how to love. Your guide loves you, accepts you, despite your negativity, because your guide sees beneath the encrusted surface garbage down to the "diamond" beneath. If you want to see how loving acceptance works, simply talk to your guide and see what happens. Develop the habit of conversing mentally with your guide. The more you do, the more he or she can help you. As you learn to work with your guide, you will derive knowledge, sustenance, and strength. Here is how one young man, smarting over the pain of rejection, was able to get help from his guide.

Howard: *Somebody whom I wanted to be close with didn't want to be close with me.*

Guide: *Why not?*

Howard: *She said I was too negative, that I wasn't where she was or what she needed. She said call back in two years.*

Guide: *Why does that bother you?*

Howard: *It hurts very much to be told you're not good enough.*

Guide: *Is that what she said?*

Howard: *Not in those words, but that's what it means, doesn't it?*

Guide: *Not necessarily. Maybe the problem is hers, not yours. Maybe she's pushing you away to avoid an emotional involvement she's not mature enough to sustain. Maybe she's rejecting you to avoid being rejected herself. A lot of superior-seeming people do that.*

Howard: *How do I know which it is?*

Guide: *Does it really matter?*

Howard: *God, this all hurts, to think how I blew it. How I had no choice, because of negative love, but to blow it. I fell hard for her and was terribly lonely and couldn't help showing both to her.*

Guide: *(Putting arm around Howard's shoulder) It's all right to show people how you feel.*

Howard: *But knowing that doesn't make the hurt go away.*

Guide: *No, the hurt is part of this experience for you. You see what happened as pain so it inevitably is. Until you understand what it means to have someone say "No" to you, it will always be hurtful.*

Howard: *What do I do now?*

Guide: *Stop chasing after people who don't want or can't see what you have to offer. It's **her** loss, not yours.*

With his guide's help Howard was able to handle the pain of his rejection pattern.

Beyond helpful advice or information, the guide and sanctuary are useful in temporarily relieving other negative situations. Here's another way to use this psychic tool. Go to your sanctuary. While there, think of the situation that disturbs you. It may be a personal trait in yourself or a troubling relationship at home or at work. Whatever it is, give it a title, such as PROCRASTINATION or MY BOSS BOTHERS ME.

Now see the negative situation spelled out in large ugly black letters in the space in front of you. See your guide giving you a large, clear plastic bag. While you hold it open, your guide reaches up and one by one plucks the black letters from the ether and drops them into the bag. When all the letters are in the bag, he ties it tightly. The letters are wildly jumping around in the bag, trying to get back into your sanctuary and your mind, to bother you. The negative situation wants to distress you further, wants to get out of the bag, but the power of your guide keeps it confined.

Your guide holds out his or her hands. There are white laser-like beams protruding from the guide's fingertips. The light encircles the bag and withdraws all the energy from it. The letters lose their energy, fall to the bottom of the bag, where they die. The white light intensifies and dissolves the letters into a fine seed-like white powder. Your guide opens the bag and pours out the powder. As it hits the earth, wild flowers of all colors spring up and spell out the positive opposite of the negative situation. PROCRASTINATION has become PUNCTUALITY. Kneel down, smell and caress these lovely flowers.

To heighten the effectiveness of this process, see yourself reliving the same scene and responding to it positively. Instead of procrastinating, for example, see yourself arriving on time feeling relaxed. Experience yourself feeling peaceful about the scene and the situation. You can use this type of "recycling" mind revelation as often as you need help to deal with negative situations. Here's how a woman in the Process used this mind revelation to help herself deal with her jealousy.

> *I see my JEALOUSY angrily struggling in the sack and then miraculously stilled and then dissolved by the white light of God. The energy force field of the negativity is withdrawn from the bag by the beam, and the dust remaining in the sack is lifeless and gray. But (will wonders never cease?) this powder, sprinkled on the earth, fertilizes the earth, and up spring wildflowers of every color and fragrance. The negative is recycled into a positive. I see the words SECURE LOVE spelled out in the blossoms. Then I see myself at home waiting for my husband to arrive for dinner. I know that he cares for me and is faithful. I feel secure and confident that he is on his way home to me. I smile to myself with the anticipation of his arrival. I am awed by this process. My jealousy is gone, and*

what remains is even more faith in the powers of my guide. I feel cleansed and refreshed, as I did when he bathed me in the pure spring waters of the brook.

A woman who was having difficulty on her job had a similar experience. As she used the recycling technique daily, she found not only that her work was improving but so were her relations with her supervisor. Seeing the negative situation being transformed into a positive one has a temporary, beneficial effect and can help you cope with the problem until you are cleared of the negative traits.

Your guide can also help you in dealing with a negative person. Think of someone in your life whom you don't like but must deal with . . . Have your guide bring the person into your sanctuary . . . Your guide tells you there's a negative and positive aspect of the person. See your guide separate the positive and negative so the two aspects are standing side by side . . . See the negative, hostile, angry, fearful self . . . The guide firmly ejects this part from the sanctuary and bars the doors . . . The negative part of the person tries to get back into your sanctuary by pounding on the doors, but to no avail. There is no way the negative aspect of this person can re-enter your sanctuary. It has no choice but to walk down the tunnel to the outside where his own guide awaits to give him succor. Then you turn toward the positive part of this person. You may be surprised at what you see. Greet him. Allow yourself to experience this positive person as his real essence. You will find your negative charge dissipate. Permit his positive self to rejoin his negative self and his guide outside the tunnel. Practice this mind revelation as often as necessary to cleanse your mind and spirit of the negative people that bug you. You will find it works wonders.

To rid yourself temporarily of blocks or other negativities, try the following mind revelation. See your guide holding a large syringe. Your guide puts the end gently against your skin and painlessly withdraws a dark, ugly fluid. As the syringe fills, a label appears on it with the name of the negativity. (Such as, RESISTANCE.) After that first vial is filled, your guide hurls it into the air, where it explodes into cosmic dust. He or she then fills another, and then keeps withdrawing the negative fluid from you until it is drained completely.

Next your guide takes a syringe filled with a pure white, luminous serum, which is the antithesis of your negativity and painlessly injects your Trinity with this restorative fluid . . . Feel it flow throughout your Trinity . . . Experience the warmth and vibrance that comes from removing a negative feeling and replacing it with a positive, affirmative feeling. See your Trinity filled with the positive beauty it needs to reprogram your brain . . . Use this ejection-injection mind revelation as often as you like to help you deal with the blocks and resistances that keep you from being your complete, most realized self.

A thirty-eight-year-old housewife used this mind revelation to help her deal with stress at home. "I feel that I must keep some sort of balance around my children. I tried ejecting UPSET and IRRITATION and injecting SERENITY and KINDNESS just before they came home from school one day, and it made me feel better and more able to cope with them, so now I do it every morning before I wake them up and again in the afternoon. It really helps!" (The permanent relief came when she learned to love herself after the Process.) Then her love flowed easily without resistance to her children.

Here's how a twenty-one-year-old woman used this mind revelation.

> *I was at home last Saturday evening and feeling sort of blue. I knew it was because I had broken up with Ken a couple of weeks before, and I didn't have a date that night, but I got thinking that it really wasn't right to feel so down about it. So I had my guide withdraw a big syringe full of LONELINESS from my arm. When he threw it up in the air, and it exploded, I didn't feel much different, but he came right back and took out another one, and then another one. I hadn't realized that I was so full of my own loneliness, but it took three syringes to get it all out. Then he injected a big, warm, glowing syringe full of GOOD FEELINGS. I could actually feel them spreading throughout my body, and right away I thought about my macrame I hadn't had time to finish, and I started to feel cheerful. I got it out and had a really good time completing it.*

I've got to tell you that the next morning I still felt good when I met my friend Sherry to go hiking, and we met a couple of really nice guys on our hike, and I've got a date for next Saturday night!

The ejection-injection mind revelation can be especially helpful in recalling forgotten incidents from childhood. Have your guide use the syringe to withdraw I CAN'T REMEM-BER. Continue withdrawing it until you are completely empty of defensive forgetting. Then your guide injects into your Trinity the pure white fluid of EXCELLENT MEMORY RECALL. You will find that after a few repetitions of this mind revelation you will be helped enormously in recalling many details of the past.

The sanctuary is also the place in which mind-cleansing takes place. Years ago, I worked with a thirteen-year-old boy who was a bed wetter. His parents gave all their positive attention to his older sister, and he couldn't compete with her. To get negative attention from his parents he began to imagine monsters in the dark that frightened him. Since there is a fine line of demarcation between the realm of imagination and the psychic realm of the mind, negative psychic forces using his open imaginative channel crossed over. He soon found himself possessed by demonlike figures that frightened him every night, causing his brain to produce terrifying visions that made him lose control of his bladder. In his state of angry rebellion to his parents, he created a device for gaining negative attention that evolved as a frightening mental and physical problem.

After the boy found his "guide and sanctuary" he was able to go to his sanctuary each night before going to sleep. Together he and his guide ushered the frightening visions out of his sanctuary and out of his mind. Once his mind was cleansed of the negative forces, he stopped wetting the bed. While the guide and sanctuary rid him of bed wetting, they are not enough to de-program completely the negative love syndrome.

Although the guide and sanctuary are designed to enhance and support your positive loving self, it is important to know that the mind revelation is not a form of positive thinking. "Think positively," or "It's all in your mind" are just admonitions that create further conflict. Negativity remains buried until it is removed cathartically through reprogramming, and the mind revelations are a few of our tools used to accomplish this.

Nor does the Process involve admonitions to "Be more loving!" How can anyone obey such a command when mother and father, the two most important persons in anyone's life, didn't teach love? Without the childhood experience of love, or the love training of the Process, such an admonition results in more conflict and inner distress. The remainder of this book describes the highlights of the Process itself and how it is possible to eradicate negative love patterns. By obtaining a loving divorce from mother and father, self-love and self-acceptance are yours.

CHAPTER V

HOSTILE, BAYGULL,
OR ZOMBIE

People exhibit themselves to the world in one of three ways: Hostile, Baygull, or Zombie. The Hostiles are just what they appear to be: angry, gruff, difficult to approach, and hard to please. Getting along with them takes much energy and tact and more often than not is not worth the effort.

In direct contrast to the overt Hostile is the Baygull, appearing to be full of good humor and spirituality. (The term Baygull comes from a 1973 *New York Times'* photo satirizing Richard Bach's *Jonathan Livingston Seagull.* The photo introduces a bird named Wellington Goldfarb Baygull. While flying high above the bay, lost in the spirituality of the great gullness of Either/Or, he hit a fence projecting from the shore and plopped into the bay.) The Baygulls are goody-goodies who appear to be loving but actually feel no love either for themselves or others. They are easier to get along with than the Hostiles, since they rarely fight or disagree, but their smiles are only a mask to cover unloved emptiness. The Baygull man or woman uses surface pleasantness to drain others dry of love while giving only pseudo-love in return. Like the others, they give only to get.

Between the scowl of the Hostile and the smile of the Baygull is the blank expression of the Zombie. He is the one who goes unnoticed in the crowd by showing no emotion, positive or negative. The Zombie is the drab, lifeless person whose name you have the toughest time remembering because he's not fully "there" in any situation.

Figure 1

Taken together, the Hostile, Baygull, and Zombie types make up the Rocky Arc of Emotion (Figure 1). Most people rock crazily back and forth on the emotional arc, depending on the situation, but they tend to have a favorite face they show the world. Rocking back and forth creates much confusion and emotional instability. Under the veneer of the Baygull and Zombie lies a dormant yet live volcano of hostility. To discover your place on the Rocky Arc, consider the following two exercises.

Imagine yourself at age twenty-one in the following scenes. A young man spending his lunch hour in the park meets a young woman and they begin dating. Sexual encounters follow. After a few weeks, he invites her to share a gourmet dinner at his apartment. It's her first time in his place. When she arrives for dinner, she is pleasantly surprised at his tidy apartment and his refusal to let her help. She brings a bottle of his favorite fine wine. He kisses her tenderly and thanks her for her thoughtfulness. Offering her a seat on the sofa, he serves her a cocktail, hors d'oeuvres, and sits beside her while they chat happily. Dinner is timed correctly, and at 7:30 he seats her at the table. There is no awkwardness or wasted energy. He uncorks the wine she has brought and serves a gourmet meal, expertly prepared. She is amazed and delighted by his culinary skill. Each time he leaves the table to serve another course, he kisses her and tells her to sit still, he can do it himself. When dinner is completed, he says pleasantly, "You've had a tough day, darling. Go sit on the sofa and read a magazine. It won't take me long to clean up the dishes and the kitchen. I'll be with you shortly."

You are the guest. (Male readers should reverse the roles so that it is the woman who cooks for the male guest.) What would you do in this situation? Make a note of how you would respond before reading the next story.

This situation is similar to the first story. The two young people have been dating for a short time, and the woman says to him, "Why don't you come over for dinner tommorrow night at 6:30? I enjoy cooking." (If you are a woman, reverse the roles so he is cooking for you.) He thinks this is a great idea and arrives the next evening bringing a bottle of her favorite wine.

When he arrives at her apartment he finds the door ajar. He walks in and smells something burning in the kitchen. The apartment is unkept. Nylons and a girdle are on the sofa. The place appears not to have been cleaned in months. No table is set. She's talking on the telephone with a girlfriend, rehashing a party they had been to the week before. She holds her hand over the mouthpiece, says she will be with him in a few minutes, and asks him to make the drinks. After about ten minutes she hangs up the phone. She takes the drink and sits in a chair across from him rather than on the sofa next to him. Then her complaints begin. "What a lousy day I had," she groans. On and on she goes about her horrible boss, how everything went wrong, and how tired she is. The phone rings again, and it's another man inviting her for a date the next weekend. As she laughs and jokes with the caller, she turns to her guest and says, "The dishes are in the cabinet in the dining room. Do you mind setting the table? I'll be with you in a few minutes." Then she continues her phone conversation.

He gets up, finds the dishes, which have been unused for a long time, and manages to wipe the grime off them and set some sort of table. When the hostess gets off the phone, she continues with her drink. The phone rings again, and it's her mother, with whom she launches into a long, unpleasant harrangue. The guest is left sitting alone. He waits to see what will develop. Eventually she returns to him and says, "Well, let's have dinner." She serves a horrible meal. The soup is watery, the roast is burned, the potatoes are cold and lumpy. Then she says, "You didn't want any dessert, did you?" (She knows he loves desserts.) She adds, "I've stopped drinking coffee, and you should stop, too." So no coffee is served, although he would have liked his after-dinner coffee. Soon she yawns and says, "Gee, I'm so tired. I'm going to lie down for a few minutes. Do you mind doing the dishes for me?"

What would you do as the guest? Note your gut-level response before reading on.

How people respond to these stories is indicative of where they are on the Rocky Arc. The host or hostess in the stories represents your parents and their treatment of you. The guest's reactions show how you responded to their positive and negative treatment, and how you are continuing to react even now. The loving response to the first story would be to return the warm devotion you have received by gently persuading your host (or hostess) that you wish to continue being together and share the cleanup work. To respond this way shows that when mother and father treated you well as a child, you responded in kind.

There is no love in the second story. The self-loving response to the host's mistreatment is to withdraw calmly as soon as the situation becomes apparent, while feeling neither guilty for taking care of yourself nor angry for the unexpected turn of events. Such healthy emotional responses are rare, because of our negative parental programming.

To demonstrate this, the following sample responses to the two dinner stories come from the notes of three persons in the Quadrinity Process.

"What would I do?" wrote Nancy, a twenty-seven-year-old executive secretary who is a Hostile. "I'd let 'golden boy' do the dishes while I rested. I wouldn't be at all uncomfortable about it, but he's so good at handling everything that I'd probably just get in his way if I insisted on helping."

Her sarcasm and hostility are evident from the beginning of Nancy's answer. When mother and father treated her well, she obeyed, although she quickly turned it into an excuse to put down both them and herself. To the second, highly negative story she wrote, "I'd like to say that I'd have poured the dishwater over the selfish jerk. But I'd probably have just walked out, too angry to say anything at all to him."

When Nancy was treated badly as a child, she rebelled by sulking and going off by herself. Although she knows there's no love available, she dares not vent her anger for fear of losing in a confrontation. She was both a covert and overt Hostile.

In contrast to Nancy's hostility is the Zombie response of Chris, a forty-six-year-old psychologist.

"My first reaction (to the offer to rest while the hostess cleans up after dinner) is 'Great. Thanks. I'll wait on the couch.' My second reaction is to volunteer to help her, a probably enjoyable experience for both of us."

His terse comments and lack of emotion are typical of Zombies, who are giving the minimum to others while holding themselves in. To the second, highly negative story he wrote:

"My first reaction is, 'No, I won't do the dishes alone. But if we do them together, it'll get done fast.' With any encouragement I would explain how her actions have made me feel: hurt, uncared for, used, and cheated."

Here Chris shifts somewhat toward Baygull obedience. He's following her lead instead of taking the initiative against her abuse of him. He rebels by refusing to do the dishes alone, but quickly retreats from it and covers it with an offer of appeasement. He's still hoping he can bring her around to giving him some show of love despite her already clear rejection of him.

On the other end of the Rocky Arc is Laura, a thirty-five-year-old real estate saleswoman. She's a Baygull with latent Hostile tendencies.

> *What's my reaction? I would have sat down as he suggested. But instead of relaxing, I would have tried to figure out how I felt about him. What kind of "after dinner entertainment" did he want? Did I want to go to bed with him? Mostly my thought would be on trying to puzzle out whether he was expecting it as his reward, in which case I wouldn't do it.*
>
> *In the second story I would have tried valiantly to make a plausible excuse to leave or escape, always smiling and being very polite but angry and resentful. I'm afraid I might have stayed to do the dishes, though, as long as I was fairly sure he wouldn't try to maul me to complete the rotten evening.*

Her response to the dinner stories shows that Laura was so

manipulated as a child that she cannot respond to the loving treatment in the first story except with suspicion and confusion. She cannot believe anyone would be nice to her except with an ulterior motive. The story specifically states they were already having sex, but she still worries about it. By doing what her host tells her, she shows she was an obedient child when her parents treated her well. The second story shows that no matter how badly she was treated, she would stick around with a fake smile on her face, hoping for a crumb of love. Her angry rebellion was covered by her need (like mother) to maintain a pleasant appearance at all costs.

Where are you on the Rocky Arc of Emotion? Are you the angry Hostile, the smiling Baygull, or the emotionally dead Zombie? Perhaps you are some combination of the three, rocking dizzily back and forth. Your response to the two stories shows not only your place on the Arc, but how you responded to the kind of programming you received as a child.

Since negative love programming is only yours by adoption, you can learn to drop it. The first step toward freedom is to re-experience how and when you adopted it from your parents during your first thirteen years of life, or up to the age of puberty when physiologically childhood ends and adulthood begins.

Learning to love in the Quadrinity Process requires a series of six stages. The first stage is the Prosecution of Mother, in which you recall and relive emotionally the anger for the wrongs she did to you. It is a complete, overwhelmingly intense purging of every bit of negative feeling toward mother both expressed or unexpressed. Head trips don't do it.

The second stage, the Defense of Mother, holds an equally important truth. Mother was once a child herself and was also programmed. Knowing this intellectually isn't enough to break the grip of the programming. It must be seen and experienced emotionally in order to arrive at a truly compassionate understanding of mother's tragedy of lovelessness. With emotional understanding and no condemnation and compassion, mother is absolved, and the childhood hostility to her totally disappears. After the Defense of Mother, it becomes possible to begin dropping the negativities you adopted from her and to replace them with the emerging positive patterns of your spiritual self.

The same two-stage procedure is experienced with father. He, too, must first be prosecuted for his sins of omission and commission. It is impossible to defend him truly until he has first been thoroughly prosecuted for his part in the negative love programming. When the anger is spent, he appears as just another programmed little boy grown old but not up. His defense, like mother's, requires seeing and emotionally experiencing how he was an unwitting victim of the negative love syndrome and helplessly passed the disease along to his children. After his defense, his negative traits begin to lose their grip and can be recycled to their positive opposites. (Step-parents, foster parents, other relatives or surrogate parents *must* also be prosecuted and defended.)

The four stages of the Prosecution and Defense of Mother and Father allows the client to take a powerful step toward freedom and autonomy. The next step after ending the war with the parents is to end the war between the negative emotional child and the intellect. When you find yourself thinking one way while acting another, you are experiencing the effects of this internal conflict. This fifth stage of the Process consists of a confrontation between the present-day intellect and the poor programmed negative emotional child. They both vent their mutual hostility and after discovering that both are blameless, a state of truce is reached.

The final resolution of all internal conflict and the reintegration of the fragmented Quadrinity take place in the sixth stage, known as Closure. It is a re-birthday. The loving divorce from mother and father takes place. This allows your true, mature self to emerge. Closure is the ultimate goal toward which the entire Process is directed. It is a confirmation of the fact that your essence is positive and loving.

The Prosecution of Mother begins with recalling her negative traits and the childhood incidents in which they were expressed. In the Process we use a list of negative traits, moods, and admonitions to help clients clarify their thoughts and recollections about mother's negativity. The entire list runs to five hundred different traits, moods, and admonitions, both silent and overt, clustered under more than a dozen major headings. For example, under the cluster heading Uncaring/Nonsupportive are dozens of such specifics as:

1. Cold

2. Neglectful

3. Not loving

4. Insensitivity in relationships

5. Non-supportive

6. Inconsiderate

7. Stingy

8. Selfish

9. Disrespect toward spouse and children

10. Invalidater of others

11. Stubborn—resistant

12. Martyr—poor me

13. Moods: I don't have time for you.

14. I am more important than you.

15. Admonitions: Your feelings are not important. Children should be seen and not heard.

16. You will never amount to anything.

17. No one will ever like you, etc.

The general negative love patterns described in Chapter 2 are composed of how we respond to specific traits such as these, whether we adopt them or rebel against them. It is not unusual to find as many as several hundred traits, moods, and admonitions that mother exhibited during your childhood. Each is a potential source of adult despair and unhappiness. (Father's traits are the other source of negativity and are considered after the mother's work is completed, when father is prosecuted. If mother's and father's traits are incompatible, this conflict in itself is another cause of confusion and emotional instability.)

In the next chapter we will present the Mother Prosecution work of three clients who were introduced in the Rocky Arc Discussion. Nancy (a Hostile), Chris (a Zombie), and Laura (a Baygull). Their own natural sensory perception abilities plus mind revelations enabled them to answer many early life questions. Clients who later check out what they have sensed are usually amazed at the high level of accuracy of their psychic receptions. In order to do their work with full impact we helped them become aware of the different kinds of mothering and recognize their own particular deprivations by posing the following rude questions.

Did your mother want you? How did she feel about being pregnant? How did she feel about your father during her pregnancy? Were you the sex mother wanted? If not, mother may have pushed you away, felt guilty about the rejection, and then smothered you with compensatory guilt-love to hide her true feelings about you. If you are the wrong sex in mother's eyes, her invalidation and rejection of you began the day you were born.

Did you feel *really* loved by mother? Or did she treat you as another burden, when she already had too much to handle? Did she ignore you or relegate your upbringing to older children or relatives? Was she there for you when you needed her? If she died or deserted you before your puberty, she cheated you of your right to a consistent flow of mother's love. The child within you is still angry with mother for leaving, whatever the cause or explanation. *She left, and you lost a mother's love.*

How did mother demonstrate her love? Did she take time from her schedule to spend a few quiet moments with you? Or was she so absorbed in her own activities that you felt you were intruding if you sought her attention? Did she greet you with a hug and kiss when you came through the door? Or was she off pursuing her selfish interests? It is defensive to say, "I know she loved me even if she had trouble showing it." *When do you remember being held lovingly in her arms?* There's a difference between intellectually believing you're loved and *feeling* that love surrounds you. If you *believe* but don't *feel* that she loved you, you may well suspect that she was play-acting at the role of loving mother, offering only pseudo-love.

How did mother teach you to relate to your brothers and sisters? Did she teach you to compete with all the others for the few crumbs of attention and affection she doled out? Was mother able to ease you lovingly through the transition period after the arrival of a younger child? Or were you abruptly displaced in favor of your younger brother or sister? Part of mother's responsibility is to prepare each child for the arrival of the next by including, not excluding, the older ones. The horror of sibling rivalry is not inevitable or natural. It is the direct result of mother's failure to create a loving atmosphere in which each child feels united with the others and with her.

Some mothers truly believe they prepare the older child for the younger child's birth, and it is rarely successful. To prevent the emotionally crippling experience of sibling rivalry, mother has to be a loving woman and a loving mother who is able to give for the sake of giving. Picture the following.

Mother is pregnant, and you are an only child. She takes you in her motherly arms and says, "Ron, *we're* going to have a baby! *We* are going to have a baby." She doesn't say, "I am going to have a baby," or, "Your father and I are going to have a baby." She says *we*. This includes Ron. She doesn't say, "You're going to have a brother." If Ron asks, "What's it going to be, Mom?" the mother answers, "It is going to be a boy or a girl, whatever God gives us. *We* will love it." Again, *we* will love it. Mother lets Ron feel her abdomen as the fetus grows. He feels the baby kick. With this preparation and mother's flowing *constant* love, all goes well.

As the birth approaches the child is told that mother will be away in the hospital to have our baby. She's only going to be gone a few days, and Aunt Ellen will be here to help us. When mother comes home, she'll bring *our baby* with her. The time arrives and Ron is prepared for Aunt Ellen.

Aunt Ellen takes loving care of Ron. When Daddy is home his love is real and consistent. The child *knows* that he is loved, cared for, and wanted. Ron is repeatedly reminded that the new baby in the hospital with Mommy is *our baby*, a girl named Katherine Louise. A few days later, when the infant is ready to be brought home, a nurse or friend is asked to hold the infant outside the home while mother and dad enter. Mother exclaims, "Where's my little Ron? Oh, Ron, there you are! Oh, Mommy loves you and missed you so! Come here, darling." Ron runs to mother, receiving warm affection in her arms. He is happy to see her and he feels loved, comforted, and secure. She easily transmits feelings of mother love, acceptance, and approval. The child then remembers the baby and asks, "Where is our baby?" Mother replies, "Oh, yes! We have a baby sister." The baby is then brought in and when first seen by Ron is not in mother's or father's arms. *Jealousy* is thus avoided. When the baby is brought in, mother is holding Ron on her lap. The friend or nurse then places the baby on Ron's lap while mother holds his sister. Mother caresses Ron in her arms, kissing him, fondling him, and making statements like, "Isn't our baby cute? It's our baby, sweetheart. You can kiss our baby if you want to. It's okay." The older child kisses "our" baby. Mother has transferred love to the older child and he to the baby. This continues for a while. Ron perhaps plays with the baby's tiny fingers and toes. Since he has been receiving love from mother, he doesn't feel rejected, and he is not angry and resentful of the infant. It becomes a joyous project, taking care of *our* infant. Mother might ask, "Shall we put *our* baby to sleep? Would you like to rock *our* baby?" "Would you like to help diaper *our* baby?" Variations of this scene continue for a few days.

Note that all this time mother gives love and affection to Ron as she did before the birth of the baby. He does not feel left out or unimportant. The baby is also not feeling rejected, for its older sibling transfers the mother's love to it. One day soon, however, something like this will happen. Ron will come over to Mommy after *he* has kissed and loved *our* baby and realizes, for the first time, that mother hasn't kissed *our* baby, and he says to mother, indignantly, "Mommy, *you* kiss our baby, too!" *Now* Mommy has permission to kiss, to fondle, to be affectionate, and to love *our* baby. She shares this love equally with the baby and her older son. No sibling rivalry can or will occur if she follows this pattern throughout the child-rearing days. Parents who have used it report this process is dramatically successful in preventing the scars of sibling rivalry.

Unfortunately, what usually happens after a baby is born

is something like this: The baby is brought home in mother's arms and becomes the new center of attention. The next older child turns away, filled with jealousy, anger, and insecurity. He is no longer number one, and his replacement is occupying *his* rightful place. Or, if he is programmed for goody-goody obedience, he may outwardly accept the baby while sulking and avenging his anger by secretly mistreating the infant when mother is away or not looking. The angel's halo often turns to devil's horns when the opportunity presents itself. If being nice to the younger one appears to be the way to get mother's love, he may hide his frustration and resentment behind a facade of sweetness and affection. The internal conflict remains for life. He becomes a Baygull with covert hostility.

The apparent triumph of the second child turns to emotional catastrophe if a third child appears. He loses his favored status but finds no warmth from his older brother, who continues to resent him. He in turn resents the youngest. He is sandwiched between them and often has no one to whom he can turn. The middle child suffers a terrible position. The first and third child may get along well together, however, since they are usually not rivals. The ones next in line to each other have great difficulties developing mutual love and trust unless mother has enough love for each of them, which rarely happens.

If you had an older brother or sister, recall what it was like. Were you loving friends, or hostile enemies? Perhaps you wanted to be loved and accepted by your older sibling, but he only played with you until friends of his own age came around. Then you were ignored, teased or bullied. While you may have been hurt and resentful toward your brother or sister, the cruel treatment was really mother's fault. Had she prepared the older one properly for your arrival and not slighted her or him after your birth, the tragedy of sibling rivalry could have been avoided. Your older sister or brother was as much a victim as you were. Each of you lost out on the experience of sibling love because of mother's ineptness.

What was your first day of school like? Did mother help you prepare for this new adventure of learning? Or did she see school as a way to get rid of you for a few hours while she attended to your younger rivals at home? Did she take you to school and warmly reassure you that you weren't being abandoned to hostile strangers? Did she really care about what you were doing in school? How did she respond when you brought home report cards, how did she treat you? Was she indifferent to your progress? Did she always criticize without adding any praise for achievement? Were expectations of grades too high? Did she make you feel like a failure if you weren't first in the class? Did she expect you to perform well so that she could advance herself in the eyes of her friends? Did she come to school on parents' day?

How did your mother handle the special days of the year, such as your birthday, Christmas, and other holidays? Were these occasions really joyous and festive? Or did she treat each as a domestic burden to be endured with a false smile? Were these events really family occasions? Or were they semipublic presentations in which mother "proved" what a good mother she was by showing off her household to relatives and neighbors? Was your birthday party for you or for her? Or perhaps she totally ignored your birthday? Were holiday meals prepared and served with love and warmth? Or were they joyless, dutiful affairs? How did she respond to the gifts you gave her? How do you feel about your birthday or Christmas? Do you look forward to these days with joy or do you dread them?

How did mother discipline you? Did she smack you around at the slightest provocation, teaching you to fear her anger? Or did she ignore your misdeeds and fail to give you clear guidelines for behavior? Did she give you the silent treatment to show her displeasure? Or did she ignore discipline and leave it to your father? Did she have a sense of justice, making the "punishment fit the crime"? Did she help you feel loved even while temporarily withholding a privilege? Or did she teach you to be afraid of admitting a mistake? Or did she show you that errors are the natural way we all learn?

A child will always test mother's love through misbehavior. In parental response, the three basic forms of discipline usually exhibited are: (1) the cast-iron fist of harsh discipline; (2) the limp wrist of indecisive discipline, and (3) the firm hand of loving discipline. The following is an example of the first discipline, the cast-iron fist. Mother is working in the home. The child wants attention or perhaps wants to get even with mother for loving the baby instead of him. He knocks down one of mother's favorite vases. Mother sees it happen, is furious, and spanks the boy. "You naughty child! Look what you've done! You've broken mother's favorite vase. Go to your room. First give me those comic books. And there's no television for three days! You're a miserable brat!" This is followed by a few more slaps. The child goes to his room and cries, "Mommy doesn't love me, and I hate her, too!" He had tested mother, found her wanting, and now has a legitimate reason to hate her.

If mother follows the limp wrist type of discipline, she will see the broken vase and say in a Zombie tone of voice, "Oh, Ron, why did you do that? Now run along outside and play somewhere else, dear." She then sweeps up the mess and throws it in the garbage. The child is left in limbo. He doesn't know what to expect. The child doesn't know if he's cared for or not because there was *no* response from mother. He learned that she is a *care-less* mother. He is unimportant. He doesn't count and isn't worthy even of negative attention.

The third and correct way of disciplining a child is with the firm hand of love. When the vase is dropped, mother speaks in a firm but not angry tone of voice, "Ron, you broke my vase purposely." Ron says, "Mom, I didn't mean to." Mother continues in an even tone of voice, "But I saw you do it, Ron." "But, Mom . . . " Mother responds calmly but directly, "I saw you do it, and I love you too much, Son, to permit you to destroy someone else's property. Since you did do it on purpose, you have to accept the consequences. Hand me those comic books. There will be no television for three days. Now, go to your room." Ron, whimpering: "Mom, I didn't mean to." Mother, "Oh, but you did do it, and you have to learn right from wrong. But first come here. Son." Mother takes Ron in her arms and says quietly and lovingly, "You have to be punished, and Mother loves you." She kisses him and tells him to run along. As Ron goes to his room accepting his just punishment, he smiles to himself. "Mother loves me." He plays in his room until punishment. time is over. He is secure in his knowledge of mother's consistent love. He has tested mother and not found her wanting. He learned the difference between right and wrong, with love. Did your mother discipline you this way?

How did she handle your illnesses? Did she make you feel guilty for getting sick and disrupting her routine? Or did your illnesses make her anxious and nervous? Did she teach you that getting sick was the only way to get her sympathetic, tender attention? Did she know how to handle your needs with intelligence and understanding? Or did she become confused and helpless?

Mother's attitude toward your father was your first lesson in how women relate to men. Did she respect and understand your father? Did she lovingly greet him when he came home? Did she hold him up to you as a worthy example of manhood? Or did she run him down, criticizing and emasculating him so that you learned women are shrews, and men are no good? Was mother an equal to your father, sharing with him in making important decisions affecting the family? Or was she his frightened victim, obediently taking orders? What example did she set?

How did mother treat your friends? Was she jealous of their time with you? Did she force children on you in order to keep you occupied? Did she choose your friends for you, thus teaching you not to trust your own judgment about people? Or did she allow you to choose your own while letting you know she disapproved of your choices? Were certain groups of people unacceptable as potential friends? If so, mother planted the seeds of your adult prejudices.

Did mother have a sense of humor? Was laughter important in her life? When she laughed, was it with genuine enjoyment and pleasure? Above all, did she teach you how to see the lighter side of life's inevitable problems and difficulties? Or was she so caught up in anxiety or anger that there was no room for amusement? If mother didn't teach you to laugh, she cheated you of one of life's best free remedies against despair and self-hatred. For that alone she deserves to be prosecuted.

The day of your first menstruation or seminal discharge is the second most important day of your life, after the day of your birth. It is the date of physiological adulthood; the day childhood is left behind. (The third most important day occurs when your body dies.) The onset of puberty marks the end of childhood and its negative love programming. The rest of life is spent replaying the tapes (unless something is done to erase the tapes and make new ones). If mother programmed you negatively about your sexuality, she cheated you of the enjoyment of love's most magnificient physical expression. What kind of send-off did your mother give you? Was she frank without being callous? Did she tenderly give you the information and guidance you needed? Did mother help you *celebrate* your emergence into adulthood?

In recalling your childhood with mother, keep in mind that her acts of omission are most vital. Often people will say, "Mother never said anything about . . . " Although there may have been no painful trauma, the memories of what she didn't do has thoroughly negative effects. Whatever was missing that would have made for a complete mother-child relationship is evidence against her. If you have difficulty recalling much of your relationship with mother, remember that we tend defensively to forget the painful incidents from the past. One of the tragedies of negative love patterns is that we continue to live the programming while forgetting and blocking its origins. The purpose of recalling mother's negative traits and the scenes in which she expressed them is to learn that we became our negative selves by emulating her or rebelling against her.

Once the traits are recorded and the scenes are "relived" it is possible to write the story of the childhood relationship with mother from the negative perspective. In the Process we call it the Negative Emotional Autobiography with Mother. Writing out the memories and the emotions attached to them helps clarify the merging picture of mother's covert and overt negativities which she passed on to her innocent children in the form of negative love. Seeing her from this perspective is an important preparation for the emotional catharsis that follows in the bitch session process. Getting through the negative programming requires an act of overt rebellion against the bitch aspect of mother, not her positive spiritual self. The hostility must spew forth like an exploding volcano. This can't be done just by screaming or raving, "Poor me! Poor me!" The angry feelings must be directed where they belong: at the mother who failed you in the worst possible way by not providing a consistent flow of nourishing love.

The overt Hostile vents his anger easily during the Prosecution of Mother. He comes into the Process knowing he's angry at everyone, including his parents, without really understanding why. In his hostility he has turned her rejection of him into his rejection of others. With mother's negative trait list and the negative emotional autobiography, he is able to redirect and focus his anger on its real source, his unloving mother.

Some people, particularly the Baygull goody-goodies, complain that they can't bitch at mother, or later at father, because of the Biblical commandment to "honor thy father and mother." The best way to honor mother and father is by doing for yourself what they were unable to do for you. Once you learn to love yourself and others, you can be a far better and loving son or daughter than you ever will be if you remain chained to them with negative love. Thus the bitch session is the first step to real, not phony, honor for mother. A Quadrinity Process premise is that out of every negative comes a positive.

People on heavy religious, meditation, or spiritual trips have trouble bitching at mother because they feel they have *already* forgiven her. Their rationale for holding back their true feelings of anger and contempt for mother is expressed something like this: "See, Mother, how I've grown and matured? I'm above all that anger and resentment from the past. I forgave you long ago." Are you sure you've thoroughly forgiven mother? If you have, (1) she can no longer have a negative effect on you and it's delightful to be with her; (2) you are no longer emulating her negative traits.

The Baygulls sometime commiserate with mother: "Poor Mommy. I won't let these people abuse you and put you down this way. I know you tried hard. You won't love me if I let them put you down. So I'll protect you, don't worry." Permitting the client to cling to this self-deception would allow him to lose the war against the effects of his negative love programming. If there is no emotional purging of the deeper anger towards mother, there can be no genuine reintegration of the four parts ot the Quadrinity. The smiling Baygull must be made to realize that feeling and expressing the expressed anger is the only way to deal with it.

With Zombies, the problem is often even more difficult. They have been programmed to feel nothing. The older and deader they are, the more difficult it is to break down their defense. Once open, though, they bitch all the more violently for the years of emotional paralysis and deadness.

Whatever the excuse, it must be confronted and negated. Genuine compassion and understanding with no condemnation, the vital intermediate steps toward learning to love, can only be achieved by first cleaning out the festering disease. Again and again this point is driven home until everyone, Hostile, Baygull, and Zombie, understands that the only way to attain peace with mother is to go to war with her in the bitch session.

The bitch session itself is unlike the earlier Process sessions. Initially, clients take notes on the information in the lecture, while reserving the expression of their mind revelations and inner experiences for the one-to-one work with their personal teacher. The group meetings are not encounter style. Questions are asked, but the interaction between client and teacher occurs through the written notes, the tape-recorded feedback, and also teacher-client sessions as needed.

On bitch night the anger that will cleanse them of the negative love programming, and give them permission to rebel against it totally, needs to be fully and cathartically expressed. This results in a declaration of independence and autonomy. Individuals are asked to wear comfortable clothing, permitting complete freedom of movement. Each brings a large pillow to represent mother.

Teachers assist their clients with the bitching. We encourage the use of street language and curse words because they have great therapeutic shock value and promote gut-level emotional bitching.

At this point, the week of work on mother's negative trait list and the negative emotional autobiography pays off. The shock is powerful when everyone is made to see that by adopting her negativities through negative love they became that bitch mother *all over again.* They recognize the source of their life-long discontent, distress, and misery is none other than the bitch mother who failed them so miserably and with such devastating consequences. After a mind revelation to prime the anger and intensify the pressure, each is instructed to "put mother on the pillow" and confront her with words, fists, and foam bats, permitting the explosion to take place.

There is no sound quite like the din of thirty men and women settling the old scores with mother. With total lack of restraint and animal-like fury, they let her have it for all the lies, put-downs, abuses, injustices, and denials from childhood, including the worst sin of all: not loving. Each person is allowed to bitch at mother until a feeling of freedom is reached. It is crucial that they continue to bitch until they break through to uncontrollable, visceral anger. In the Process such screaming anger is done with dispatch. Clients do not have to scream for months and years. This may take several hours. No one is allowed to fail the bitch session and if necessary further help is given.

Following the evening bitch session, clients are advised to take a tape recorder to the woods the next day, find a large rock, and chalk mother's picture on it. They throw stones while experiencing and taping a second bitch session. This second bitch session reinforces the first and provides further release for the years of pent-up anger and resentment. The purpose is to drain off residual anger. The tape is later reviewed by the tacher to ensure that the bitching work has been completed with no pockets of anger left unpurged.

At a deep level everyone is hostile toward the parents who failed to teach them to love themselves and others. *Everyone!* Once the right button is pressed, anyone will explode. Finding the right button and knowing how to press it is something only a skillfully trained teacher can do. Rarely does one confront himself and call his own lies. It hurts too much, and it's easier to avoid looking at the truth when the exposed nerves start throbbing; the procedure is like an operation with no anesthetic, as the notes of Nancy, Chris, and Laura in the next chapter make clear. Each experienced the pain of building to the catharsis of the bitch session against mother but afterward achieved a great sense of relief as they triumphantly claimed their autonomy and freedom from mother.

CHAPTER VI

"I HATE YOU, YOU BITCH!"

In the prosecution steps the clients understand that they arc prosecuting *only* the negative side of their parents and acknowledge that there is a positive side. For the sake of the work recognition of the positive natures of Mother and Dad are temporarily put aside.

The following notes are excerpts from the Process work of the Hostile (Nancy), the Zombie (Chris), and the Baygull (Laura). No one is a single type; the notes of each contain fragments characteristic of the others. Nancy, the Hostile, was programmed to suppress her feelings and therefore is sometimes Zombie-like, while Chris the Zombie shows some Baygull false pleasantness. Laura's Baygullism, of course, is a cover for deep hostility that only gains expression when she is free to bitch at mother.

The incidents from their childhood emotional autobiographies explain the origins of their place on the Rocky Arc of Emotion. The intensive feedback each received (presented here only in summary form) make cognizant the reality of their negative love attachment to mother. As Chris so aptly put it, "I can't believe it! I am my *mother!*"

While the negative emotional autobiography tells the story of the client's childhood relationship with mother, it is not a case history in the usual sense. The purpose of the negative emotional autobiography with mother, and later with father, is for the client to experience how his current negative behavior patterns result directly from the adoption of negative patterns of his mother and father. It is not enough to say, "You are the way you are because of the way your parents were." While obviously true, such a statement is of no help to the person who wishes to be free of his parents' negative influence. The negative emotional autobiography provides not only the specifics of the individual negative traits but goes beyond that to express, in the client's own words, the scenes from his childhood in which he saw, heard, and felt mother or father expressing the traits. It is the clearest possible demonstration of the negative love syndrome in action, and it never fails to yield genuine understanding of the life problems.

If the client resists the work, for example, by putting the teacher down while attempting to prove himself right, it is a simple matter to consult the negative trait list of mother or father and find the traits of "putting others down," "invalidated new ideas," and "had to be right all the time." Whenever examples like this come up, the client's awareness is directed to the negative trait list so that he fully understands the origin and meaning of his negative response: negative love to mother and father. With the dramatic, emotional experience of his positive spiritual self, the client is ready to move on.

Although everyone in the Process suffers from the disease of negative love, each is afflicted in his own way. These differences and similarities are apparent in the three sets of notes that follow. As you experience these three people working through their negative love patterns in preparation for the later stages of the Process work, you will undoubtedly gain insights into your own life. Although not a do-it-yourself volume, the remainder of this book will be something like watching a good friend discovering his positive essence. Carefully observing the procedure will increase your knowledge of the problem and its solution and help you on your way.

NANCY, THE HOSTILE-ZOMBIE

Nancy is a tall, slender woman of twenty-seven. Her otherwise attractive appearance was marred by her slumped carriage and sullen expression. Alone with two small children after two broken marriages, she was aware that she had chosen unstable men who shared her inability to sustain an intimate relationship. Her work as a secretary left her frustrated and bored, but she could not decide what to do to change her life. She felt powerless to break free of her negative patterns despite her repeated efforts and encouragement from her few friends.

The following excerpts from Nancy's negative emotional autobiography with mother show how her mother taught her to be both hostile and emotionally unexpressive. (Her father's contributions to her emotional problems are recounted later.) The autobiography covers the period of birth through puberty. Nancy wrote:

When I was born, my mother expected that I'd make up for all the disappointment and unhappiness in her life. Father was away a lot and didn't pay much attention to her when he was home. She really hated men. She thought they'd made things so hard for her. She figured my brothers belonged to my father, but that I didn't. She kept me away from him right from the beginning. She never really forgave either of my brothers for the hard time she had giving birth to them. She kept telling them what a good baby I was. Of course, they didn't like that, and they didn't like me much, either. All I wanted was to be loved and nourished, not to be used in her battles!

We moved to another town when I was about three, and my mother told me we were only going to be there for a little while until my father would join us, so I kept waiting and looking for him, but he didn't come. I got madder and madder at her. She never wanted me to have a daddy. She took us away. Soon she started working in a restaurant downstairs from our apartment. My brothers went off by themselves most of the time, so I was alone with no one to take care of me. I was furious at her for taking me away from Daddy and then for leaving herself, but I was afraid to let her know. She'd get angry at me which always gave her an excuse to take off and leave me alone. I played with one little boy who was a year younger than me. Sometimes he was mean and tore my comic books. When I went running to tell my mother, she said I was a big girl and shouldn't complain, and she laughed about how cute he was. And I felt mean and ugly toward her, and that scared me even worse, so I tried to stop feeling anything at all.

When I was about six, we moved back with my father for about six months. My mother was often in tears and angry, and they fought a lot. Once I heard her scream at him, "God will strike you dead for what you have done!" I was terrified and kept expecting a lightning bolt to hit us. My brothers stayed away from the house as much as they could, but I was too young to go anyplace, so I just hung around, feeling terrible, not understanding their fights and bitterness. We were all miserable, and she had brought us there. She made me behave politely to him while making it clear he was a bad man doing terrible things. I learned later he left us to live with another woman, but she didn't tell me anything at all about that. All I knew from her was that my daddy hated us.

Soon we moved again, away from my father, to a house in the country. We were three miles from the nearest town. Our one friend, who came occasionally with a car and goodies, was the relative who owned the house, an old man we called Uncle Teddy. I loved the attention I got from him. But I dreaded the way he touched me. Once I gathered up my courage and mumbled to my mother that Uncle Teddy was putting his hands inside my panties. She got hysterical, which made me terribly frightened. I felt as if I had done something shameful. She ordered me to tell her if he did it again. The next time he came over, she asked me if it had happened again. I lied, saying it had not, because I was so afraid of getting her all upset again. I felt angry and resentful that she hadn't protected me and scared because I couldn't depend on her.

Once a neighbor offered me fifty cents to drown three baby kittens. I'd watched my mother chop the heads off chickens, and my brothers shot game. It seemed like an OK way to make some money. My mother shamed me when she heard about it, making me feel as if I were inhuman and wicked. I felt confused and resentful, and terribly ashamed and bad. Anything I did was likely to turn out to be a bad thing. I became afraid to act.

About that time I became repelled at her body. She was soft and flabby, her underwear was ugly, and she was often sweaty, and I hated her body odor. When she tried to hold me, I stiffened. I didn't pull away because then she'd have asked me why, and I wouldn't have dared to tell her the truth. So I tried to control the pulling away and forced myself to pretend to hug back.

She believed it necessary to empty one's plate and forced me to eat food that sickened me. Creamed spinach was the worst. She'd give me a big portion, and then she'd eat a few tablespoons from my plate so that I wouldn't have so much of it to eat. I knew that she wanted me to appreciate her taking some away, but she'd put it there in the first place. That confused me because I felt angry and terribly relieved at the same time.

When I was nine, we moved to a town in Connecticut. My mother took us to a horror movie. It literally terrified me, and I hid under the seats, peeping out from between them. She was angry at me for "acting up." At the end of the show I pleaded with her to see it through again. Somehow I knew that if I could see it knowing how it ended, it would take some of the poison of terror away. As usual, she treated my serious request with contempt, sneering at me for having been so frightened, not understanding what I was asking for. All night long I would reach over and feel her fingernails to see if she were growing claws like the beast in the movie. I had to get up to pee repeatedly, and my pajamas were wet with the cold sweat of fear. Here she was, my own mother, and instead of being a haven of security, I imagined that she might turn into the savage, murderous beast!

When I was twelve, I was elected editor of the class newspaper. This was special because it was very unusual for me to get positive notice from the other kids. When I told her they called me the "gossip columnist" of the class she looked disgusted and said she wouldn't want me to be that kind of person. I felt angry and resentful but as always said nothing to her. Again she had destroyed my smallest pleasure in relating to other children.

It was during this time, too, that she left a pamphlet on menstruation out where I would see it but could not bring herself to mention the subject to me. Again I felt a flash of resentment. I wanted her to talk to me about sex, to make it less strange and frightening, but she couldn't handle that, either.

My first menstrual period had no meaning for me. I went through it as I had learned to go through anything unpleasant—by turning off my connections with myself and simply watching as if it were happening to someone else.

Nancy's first menstrual period marked the onset of her puberty and the end of her negative love programming. She received a lengthy, paragraph-by-paragraph response to her Negative Emotional Autobiography on tape cassette. The hostility she had learned became overt during her teenage years and was obvious in her sullenness and difficulty in relationships as an adult. At this point in the Process it was necessary for her to experience hostility fully and direct it to her mother (though, *not* in person). After each paragraph I would comment indignantly. "So mother's already teaching you men are no good. Look at all the relationships with men you had to break with in order to obey *that* negative trait. Two husbands and you are only twenty-seven! "I pointed out how her mother had created and encouraged the sibling rivalry that had cheated her of her brothers' love. I asked her what had happened to *them* because of the bitch mother, and her knowledge of their devastated adult lives (I knew they had to be) heaped fuel on her rage.

I supported her perceptions of how she had been taught to ignore and smother her own emotional responses, of how hard she had tried to learn to be a "good girl" to win the love

of her unloving mother. I refused to let her blame her father
at this point (his turn would come), but kept her focused on
her mother's responsibility in driving him away and creating
a miserable home life. Angrily she saw clearly how unde-
pendable her mother's so-called love was, how she had been
on a seesaw and never knew where she stood. Her mother
was only concerned with her own feelings, scaring the young
Nancy with her own hysteria while neglecting her responsibility to comfort and support the child when the old man
(Uncle Teddy) sexually molested her.

Again and again I castigated her mother and drew Nancy's
attention to what she was beginning to see: how the negative
traits of her mother—angry, putting men down, unloving, uncaring, feeling superior, nonsupportive, unwilling to face
reality, on and on through the 276 she had listed—had
actually become her own by adoption through negative love.

When she described her reaction to the horror movie incident, I assured her she was correct in seeing her mother as a
murderous beast who might turn and claw her. In the bitch
session her turn came to avenge herself against this woman
who had all but destroyed her by programming her to be a
Hostile-Zombie.

Simply bitching at mother, however, is not sufficient.
Nancy's anger had to be *directed* to the particular behaviors
and attitudes of mother which she adopted into her own personality. To help her see this, she was asked to review her
list of mother's negative traits and decide for each if she
adopted it out of negative love to mother or rebelled against
it, creating more conflict. A potent mind revelation was experienced to eliminate defensiveness. With shock, she recognized that she was her mother the bitch all over again. While
the recognition is painful, it serves the vital purpose of further priming the pump of anger for the bitch session that
follows. Nancy had little trouble with this since she was more
than ready to let her mother have it. It was her declaration of
independence from mother's negative traits.

Here is Nancy's description of her supervised bitch session,
done in the safety of our center and using a large pillow to
represent mother:

> *From my first words it was as if something took
> over inside me. I saw my mother—immobilized by*

my guide in my sanctuary—trying to control me with her eyes, looking enraged and warningly at me. And I flashed on the times that people have said to me that I had just such a black look. She herself had accused me of that. At that moment I started feeling real anger. I called her a "fucking hysterical bitch" and hit the pillow as hard as I could with the bat. My voice startled me—it was almost a scream. I kept yelling, "You stupid, stupid bitch!" and hitting with the bat. I kept coming back to, "Do you know what you did to me, you stupid bitch?"

I was saying things to her I had never been able to say before—how she had, quite literally, destroyed my brothers, how she had warped my whole feelings about men and about myself, how I had to spend my whole life trying not to be like her—trying to tear her out of myself.

At one point I felt like she was looming over me, blotting out the whole world with her image, and I wanted to beat her down to normal size. (I kept hitting with the bat all this time with all my strength. Bob thrust some Kleenex into my hand, and I realized that my eyes and nose were streaming.) I kept yelling at her, 'You're just a normal-sized woman! You're not all that big! I could literally see that huge image shrinking, as I kept beating at it.

Several times I felt exhausted and waited to see if I were finished, and then some new accusation would start boiling up inside. Then I'd go back to hitting and screaming, "You stupid bitch!" I accused her of blinding herself with rage, of being totally self-involved, hating me, driving my father away, not really loving anyone, feeling superior to other people, and at the same time being a fucking servant to them. Each time I spat out an indictment I immediately saw myself doing the same rotten thing she did and I got a spurt of renewed rage.

Afterwards I felt totally exhausted and clean. It took five minutes to straighten my knees. I never noticed the pain while I was bitching at her and beating the pillows. I felt quieter inside and softer and relieved that the blocks were broken through. I felt an exhilirating flow of life inside me.

After the session I felt that mother had been reduced to a normal-sized woman. Her neuroticism, her hysterical rages, her suffering, had always been larger than life. I began to see her as just a person (perhaps see myself as just a person), her tragedies no longer great, overwhelming disasters, her rages no longer to be feared like cataclysms. I felt as if some invisible mold that was holding me into a certain shape, "Don't be open, don't be like other people, be aloof, remember, you're better than all that (all of them)," had been shattered.

Nancy did a few bitch sessions at home and in the woods until her fury was finally spent. She felt both exhausted and cleansed, for she had had an emotional cathartic purging that reached into the center of her being. She felt totally separate from her mother, no longer needing or wanting anything to do with her. Twenty-seven years of festering garbage and decay had been removed. She was now ready to take the next step, in the Defense section, of coming to understanding mother without condemnation.

CHRIS, THE ZOMBIE

As a psychologist with years of experience in various therapies, Chris had a clear intellectual understanding of his problems. Yet at age forty-six his usually immobile features and the stiffness of his body indicated his "progress" had been mainly in the intellectual realm. He understood his inner deadness, the aridity of his relationships, and his occasional severe depressions but was unable to help his negative emotional self. He wrote:

I was born in the middle of the night to a mother who wanted me to fulfill her role as mother and wife. Duty always came first, and she would put herself or her feelings down if they didn't fit her preconceptions. Being duty bound, she did every-

thing by the book. She fed me by the clock because the book said to. I was forced to her mold quite early and conformed readily. My feelings and needs were hardly even existent unless the pediatrician or baby book said so.

I recall being dropped in a Bathinette during infancy. My mother let my head fall under water while I gasped and choked on the water, scared and hurt. Lesson number 1: I may be dependent for my existence on Mom, but I sure can't always trust her.

From very early Mother was very busy with clubs, charities, and travel. I remember at the age of two, sister Anne (age five) and I were dumped with a woman for weeks—I don't know how many. I do remember not wanting mother to leave and being taken to the backyard where there were toys, swings, etc., while she gave the lady instructions. When I came back inside, she had gone. Both Anne and I got the flu and were sick during her absence. I was so confused when she returned I'm not sure I was even glad to see her. Lesson number 1 reinforced, as well as number 2: I'm essentially powerless, and number 3: My feelings are not important.

Mother had many, many sayings about how to act, to feel, etc. One I remember well seemed to begin about age three. If I complained about something I got, "Be happy if you can, cheerful if you must, and pleasant if it kills you." I cursed her many times under my breath for that one. Be phony, be perfect, show a good front to the world, don't inconvenience anyone else by my feelings, they don't count.

Whenever I would get into some situations where I was learning something new or trying something that didn't come off, she had a favorite expression for putting me down, spitefully bruising my self-esteem: "Well, I won't say I told you so." I remember this from age four on, and at least once I said, "I wish you wouldn't say, 'I told you so.' You tell me not to be nasty like that." She jumped all over me, denying that she was being nasty.

Double messages were OK if you had the power to make your denial stick. Lesson: Don't talk back or try to reason with the unreasonable, especially Mother.

Probably the most damaging and frustrating thing she did to me over many years was to directly deny that my experience was what I said it was. My statement might be something as personal as, "I don't like asparagus." She would then answer, "Of course you do, you know you do." Message: My feelings were either not important or I didn't really have the experiences I thought I had. Whenever she used to do this, I would go into instant internal rage with an urge to shout, throw things, swear, although I don't ever remember acting on this.

She used to rub my back to put me to sleep as late as ten years old, but it was usually after I asked her to. She would then say, "What's the matter, dear, aren't you feeling well?" Lesson: It's not OK to want to touch/love except when you're not feeling well.

Her nagging was the most common greeting when we would meet in the same room. "When are you going to . . . " meaning, "If I don't remind you, you aren't competent to do it." This was applied to doctor's appointments, paper route, homework, writing Christmas thank-yous, etc. My response was almost always swallowed, suppressed anger and procrastination on those things.

I came home once after being hit on the head (it later turned out to be a concussion) while a Cub Scout meeting was in progress. I told mother I wasn't feeling well and was going to lie down. She said that was fine and continued her duties as den mother. (I wanted her to dismiss the meeting and attend to me. "Hey! I'm your son—hurt, angry, rejected.")

I wish I could have seen her get really mad at least once. She often showed displeasure to me— tight lips, refusal to talk about something, but I have no recollection of her speaking ill of anyone until long after my puberty. This includes the Axis during the war. I have a vague recollection of asking her and being told, "It's not nice to think bad thoughts about other people."

Mother stayed out of any discussion of sex. I never thought much of Mother regarding sex and puritanism, but I do remember how stuffy and scared of talking about it she was. Occasionally Dad would tell an off-color joke about sex. Mother never seemed to laugh. I recall realizing something was wrong. I thought some of his jokes funny, but Mother didn't approve, so I couldn't laugh. She would say it was all right but stiffen and otherwise show she didn't approve.

Note the contrast between Chris's emotional autobiography and Nancy's. Unlike her, he coats much of his resentment with a vacillating, saccharine-sweet tone. In the feedback his current games and evasions were pointed out and related to Mommy. He began to "see" mother, and his feelings toward her, as they really were. At each opportunity I indignantly goaded and taunted him unmercifully and castigated his mother in order to arouse his deadened emotional ire and resentment.

"From your babyhood, Chris," I told him, "mother told you how to act and feel. Be pleasant if it kills you? She killed you, all right. She split you in two. You now have a negative emotional child at war with your adult intellect. You're a neurotic wreck. Your lifelong therapies have failed you. For this you can thank your bitch mother. You can't love yourself, your wife, your children, or anyone else in your life. Your mother killed you, all right. She is a bitch! You've become an empty emotionless Zombie just like her."

In answer to his comments about his mother's sexual attitudes I told him, "If a woman expects a son to become a sexually fulfilled man, he must have no fear of women. Your model of women is your mother. If your mother didn't speak of sex, then women must, in some way, be deficient in sex. You learned the message: Women, mothers, aren't interested in sex, they don't talk about sex with their children. All of this, Chris, comes from just one sentence you wrote, 'Mother stayed out of any discussion of sex.' That one line tells it all.

Her acts of omission were as negative as her sins of commission." And your sex life has always been unfulfilled. Thanks to Mommy!

I also asked Chris to tell me how much he trusted his wife. Was his wife a reflection of mother, who had him on a seesaw of love, sometimes up, sometimes down? Here's his answer:

"No, I do not trust my wife very much with my feelings and have been much afraid of her. I have trusted her from time to time and often been disappointed. I do trust several other women. My closest friends are women, in terms of trust, but not in terms of time spent with them."

Every woman in a close relationship represents Mama in some way. A wife, especially to a man who isn't emotionally mature, is always a mother figure. The same applies to women in their relations with men. The husband is the father figure.

Because of his negative love pattern with his mother, Chris couldn't possibly trust his wife. Although his closest friends are women, he doesn't see them often. If he doesn't spend much time with them, he will have little opportunity to learn to distrust them, which is his negative pattern created by his mother. Then he won't *have* to reject them.

After my feedback Chris then wrote:

> Bob, as I worked with "negative Mother," it felt at first like a great distortion, almost like lying, to talk of the negatives without balancing them with the positives. Many of the negatives were present, true, but only part of the time. Now I have gone over and over the material, the negative is there. I do feel anger, frustration, and resentment at Mother. I have to keep redirecting it, as now I tend to turn it on myself and excuse her, which is my game, but **now** I see it.
>
> Looking at the list (of Mother's negative traits, moods, and admonitions), I went from numbness to a sense of, "I've known that before"—but **in the past,** whenever I looked, I had to look away, feeling disgust and only a flash of anger at her. (I'm not allowed to be angry.) This was followed in previous glimpses by denial, **rationalization,** or some other defense where I told myself either I wasn't really living that trait, or it was OK to be

that way. (After all, Mother is like that.)

This time I looked and saw myself expressing many of these negative traits with you, Bob. Underneath there was some stirring of feelings of self-disgust, anger at Mother, curses at the world for being like it is, and hanging on to the promise of a way out of this emotional swamp. Curious revelation: I am my mother! Gulp! Wow!

This insight Chris reached after his negative emotional autobiography is the goal toward which much of the preceding work was aimed. Chris had to see how his own most troubling problems, particularly the inability to love himself and others, came directly from the stultifying manipulations and deceits of his mother. All of what went on before was specifically to enable him to see *and feel* the impact of *"I am my mother."* After that the only thing to do was to give him room and protection while he opened the flood gates of his blocked emotions and declared his independence from mother.

The day after his supervised bitch session he wrote:

"Mother" (put that in quotes because the title is false, unearned, and the most hated of all epithets), I want you to suffer my hate. You deserve me as you've made me—afraid of people, indecisive, negative attention getter. Fuck you! I hate the You in Me. You couldn't recognize real feelings, and you taught me to ignore them. You fucked me over royally. I throw up your teaching! I want you to drown in my vomitus. Three times down and no *help—I turn my back on you and abandon you as you abandoned me.*

My throat hurts, I can hardly talk, yet I want to shout, Fuck you, Mother! You couldn't sing—so I can't sing even though I am told I can. That alone you should die for. How can any man live without singing his feelings? Croak yourself. Suffer in silence, you martyr. You had no right to hurt me this way. You fucking bitch, you've got me crying again—but now I'm going to cry for myself—never again for you and not even because of you. I won't let you stop me from feeling ever again. I'm going to feel my hatred, my anger for you. If I have to throw up and throw up, I'll do so gladly to get rid of you and your bilious, vile sourness in me. Damn you! Damn you! Damn you! I don't need injections of hate and anger. All I need is to think of you.

Where were you when I needed you? I cried in my pillow, but, you bitch, you couldn't hear 'cause you taught me to be self-sufficient. Goddamn liar! There's another of your games I took over—self-pity. I don't want your games, I don't need your games, I won't continue to play them. Hear me, Mother! I'm telling you now, I hate you, I hate your hypocrisy, I hate your phony love, your mechanical sentimental shit. I hate your fault-finding, critical, perfect fucking self right down to your rotten selfish leave-me-alone center. Take your whole nice, moral, "loving," indirect head and choke on your own shit!

You never gave me a straight message in your life. No! Now I'm so Goddamn overresponsible I can't enjoy myself. You've made me so compulsive I feel guilty all the time unless I've read everything, written everything, and done all my duties. You fucking compulsive whore!

Oh, I'm like you, all right! I'm like you right down to my fucking toes: pacifying, afraid of everything, smooth it over before it even gets going. You fucked me up thoroughly. You shut off conflict, shut off confronting—just lie down and get walked on 'cause that's the way it's supposed to be.' That's not the way it's supposed to be! *You lied about love, you lied about caring, you lied about people. You bullied and double messaged me into a shitty little scared, wishy-washy half man, half thing like you.*

(Fatigued, and shaking, I rested a few minutes. Then I closed my eyes and took a mind revelation to my sanctuary where I looked a long time at my mother tied to a stake. She was a collapsed, bleeding blob. I told my guide to throw the thing out and not let it back in unless I said to. He quickly

grabbed her, threw her bodily and roughly into the tunnel, and slammed the door.)

I'm still shaking, my whole body is tingling with a flow of energy up and down and across the entire surface of my being. I feel relieved and think I've passed some sort of milestone. Maybe I'll have to do it again, but it won't be the same. I really feel like after a race or exhausting swim. I'm at the other side now resting on the beach.

As I write this, I'm tired and yet excited, I'm not sure what I'm feeling. My mouth tastes as if I were recovering from a hangover.

P.S. (the next day): Last night I woke up at 3 A.M with the most glorious, fantastic energy vibrating throughout my whole body. I know some doors are opening to me and I eagerly await to pass through them.

The doors that were opening for Chris, like those for Nancy, lead away from the negativity he adopted from mother. He took a giant step toward becoming who he really is: a positive loving soul.

LAURA, THE BAYGULL

Nothing is as it appears to be. Laura was a small, pretty brunette who made her living selling real estate. She had a cheerful demeanor and a ready smile. Though unmarried at thirty-five, she maintained that her life was generally satisfactory. After some probing she dropped her facade. She admitted having had periods of depression and suicidal thoughts since her teen years. She also acknowledged her inability to feel comfortable in a close relationship with a man. She was aware of her considerable resentment toward her father, while believing she had been close with her mother. She saw her mother as nearly above criticism and found it hard to believe she had latent angry feelings toward her. The development of her psychic abilities in the Process permitted her to go back before her birth and re-experience the emotional truth about her mother.

When I am three months in the womb and first begin to sense things around me, I recognize that my mother is very anxious. She is pregnant with me and doesn't want to be. My father is insisting on an abortion. My mother is hurt and confused. She always submits to her husband, is dutiful, and absolutely compliant. However, he has at last asked for too much. She cannot bring herself to have an abortion. The operation is illegal, dangerous, costly, and totally unacceptable to her puritanical and religious upbringing. Her guilt would be too keen. Besides, suppose she were found out? What would people think of a married woman who did such an unspeakable thing? Because of this I am saved.

A month after she had expected me, I am finally born. It is midnight. I feel frightened by what is happening to me. I feel muscular contractions forcing me from my secret hiding place. Cold metal forceps grasp my head. I come screaming, cold, frightened, into the blinding lights and the cool, impersonal hands of the doctor, who promptly passes me to the nurse. My mother moans in her drugged state. She is barely aware of me. She focuses on her pain rather than on me. I want immediately to be reassured, fondled, breastfed, loved. Instead, I am taken to a nursery full of crying babies and left alone.

With resignation, the way she sighs and submits to unpleasant things, my mother accepts my existence and is glad I am a girl. Little girls are cute, you can dress them in sweet dresses. Mother will have a little playmate, a live doll, since she is a little girl emotionally herself. She selects the name Laura Rose for me.

I am two. My Mommy always keeps my hair curled, and I wear pink playsuits with frilly edges. But she treats me like a doll, not a living being. Even though she makes such a big deal about my being a little girl, she is anxious about the idea of my being female. She is careful not to let me see my Daddy naked. I take baths with my mother until one day I notice she has brown tits. From then on she bathes me by myself. I learn there is something wrong with having a body. It is to be covered up and ignored.

When I am three, I hear the lady next door playing the piano. It is the most beautiful sound I have ever heard. I want more than anything else to make that heavenly music. Whenever I get a chance, I strike the keys on the lady's piano. I discover that my aunt has one, too. I can't wait to go to my aunt's house. When I get there, my mother says, "Stop that noise, silly. Go off and play." I ask for a piano, but she doesn't take me seriously. At Christmas time I ask Santa Claus for a piano. My mother laughs at me and tells Santa, "You remember, Santa, how small our house is." Eventually, almost every child on the block has a piano except me. As much as I want one, my mother does not go to bat for me to see that I get one. I learn very early not to ask for those things I want most, as I know for sure that once people know what I want they will know what to take away.

She is almost always even-tempered. No matter what happens, "Everything is fine," she says. My father throws a temper tantrum, and she pretends it didn't happen. He says the same thing over and over again, and she never stops him. The weather is always sunny for my mother, and her placid smile never seems to vary. If something really unpleasant happens, she just closes her lips tight and will not talk about it. If I do something she doesn't like, she just ignores it and pretends it never happened.

One day we are in the bedroom, and my father begins to tickle my mother. She twists away from him and makes a face. He keeps right on. Mother says, "Stop. You're hurting me." My Daddy throws her on the bed. She says, "Not in front of Laura." I think Daddy is hurting her, so I pick up a comb from the dresser and throw it at him. Now both of them are mad at me for interfering. Mother doesn't like either one of us. I feel that she is unfair, refusing to understand why I threw the comb. Mother is always uncomfortable if Daddy touches her while I am around. I learn it is not nice to let a man touch you.

When I am eight my aunt in New York sends a box of books. Among the books is one about sex and babies, for children. I ask about the book, but my mother seems reluctant to let me read it. I notice where she puts it and take it out and read it. I learn that babies grow inside their mothers, although I still don't understand how they get there. One day I am sitting on the back porch with a neighbor boy while our mothers talk across the fence. I tell Donnie he was very small when he lived inside his mother. At once my mother whisks me away. My mother tells me, "I don't ever want to hear you talking about such a thing again." I feel that I have done a terrible thing and wonder whether I will be allowed to play with Donnie again. I am careful to avoid the subject of sex from then on. I learn that it is a bad thing to have a baby. Being female (or male) must also be a bad thing.

One day I give away my stuffed toys to the woman next door, who runs a day nursery. My mother cries. I feel that I must be hardhearted and cruel, so I give in to my mother's wishes and get the toys back.

During my grade school days, from time to time my mother has me come down on the bus from school and meet her at the depot. We go to the dime store for lunch, and sometimes we go to a movie. My mother makes me promise not to tell Daddy that we did these things. I can't imagine why not. I am uncomfortable about feeling sneaky. Also, I don't like thinking that fun has to be a secret and something you do when men are not around.

I learn that women are helpless. They have almost no money from their stingy husbands except grocery money, and they have to dip into this in order to have a little innocent fun. Men are ogres, and women are sweet, innocent victims!

When I am twelve, my folks buy me an accordian for Christmas. I have wanted a piano for nine years, but I get an accordion instead. My mother likes accordion music, "oldie but goodie" tunes like "Blackbird, Bye-Bye." **She** *likes the accordion. I do not. She assumes I will like the same tunes she likes. I want to learn classical music. I feel angry and resentful. I want to be a musician, not a player of pop music at afternoon teas. My mother thinks this is cute. I resent her forcing her musical taste on me.*

We often make fudge and popcorn. A whole tray of candy and a big bowl of popcorn. Overeating is a forbidden pleasure. "We'll get fat," she says. I still feel guilty whenever I eat candy.

When I am thirteen I begin to menstruate. I think perhaps I am incontinent, like my aging grandmother. With tight lips, my mother shows me how to use a Kotex and belt and tells me never to get blood on my outside clothes. I haven't any idea what this nuisance of menstruation is all about. But I know better than to ask. My mother will never speak, except by indirection, of sex.

My mother never discusses money with me. It is as taboo as sex. She never discusses her relatives. She is an ostrich; I learned to be one, too.

The clarity and detail with which Laura was able to relive her childhood allowed her to re-experience and rediscover her true feelings toward her mother. To bring her anger to fever pitch I goaded her again and again with the effects of her mother's treatment of her; how her mother had not wanted her and refused the abortion only out of self-concern for "what the neighbors would think" and the difficulties involved; how her mother had never taken her seriously as a being with needs and rights of her own; how she had cheated her out of her early love of music. I supported her perception of how her mother's attitudes toward her father and sex had shaped her own and robbed her of the ability to love a man.

I pointed out how her mother's refusal to let her grow up had created her current difficulty in functioning as an adult woman. She was shocked when she realized mother vicariously lived her own childhood through her, crying when Laura gave away her stuffed toys. She also recognized that she hated these toys because they were really mother's, not hers. Laura saw that she was *used* and was never loved for herself. I pushed her particularly hard on how her mother had taught her to fix that same placid smile on her face, which created the outward Baygull look that masked her smoldering hostility. With my response to each paragraph of her work, the facade of "always looking on the bright side," another destructive trait of mother's, began to crumble. As she examined her list of mother's 315(!) negative traits and their debilitating effect on her, she had no difficulty realizing how she had adopted mother's traits out of negative love and become mother all over again. Stripped of mother's false sweetness, she was primed and ready to give it all back to her.

Her bitch session follows:

> *I have this scared feeling. I can't do this. It's frightening. I don't think I can do it. Nothing will come out but a squeak. Then I take the preparatory mind revelation and I start. Boy, did I start.*
>
> *You fucking bitch, listen to me. I said* Listen to me! *Don't put your hands over your Goddamned ears.* Listen! *You whore, you witch! I hate you for every cold, empty, ugly way you made me feel about myself. I'm tired of being your puppet, your doll, your goody-goody on the outside and as full of shit as you are on the inside. You bore me. You're boring. You're shallow, insincere, and boring. I'm sick of not loving myself, you bitch, and feeling it was wrong to love myself because you didn't love me. You never knew who I was. All you wanted was a baby doll to dandle on your lap when company came. You didn't care about me. Well, Goddamn it,* I'm me! I'm over here! See me! *You bitch, you always put your hands over your eyes when you didn't want to see something bad.* Look at me!
>
> *You bitch, you never wanted to see me, did you? I begged you for a piano, but* you *didn't want one, so you couldn't imagine why I would want one. Because I'm me, Goddamn it, not you.* I'm not you! I don't want to be like you. I'm me! *I don't want to spend my life alone, an old maid,*

gray, colorless, and boring. I don't want to obey your admonition—don't fuck, don't enjoy, don't love, don't, don't, don't! I want to be, to do. I want positive things in my life, not the emptiness of things and people you gave me. I don't want to be invisible anymore—and I won't be! **I don't want to be an ostrich like you!** *I want to see myself as I am—an ugly bitch by adoption. But I won't be a bitch like you anymore, so take back your shit, you no-mother mother!* **Go to hell, Mommy!** *I'm sick of your compulsions, your hang-ups, your fear of living and loving. I'm sick of the garbage you put in my brain, the shit you put in my heart, the vomit you stuffed in my gut. I won't have your poison in my system anymore!*

I'm not afraid of you anymore, Mommy. All my life I've been afraid of you. "*Don't do this. Don't do that. Don't enjoy that. Be good.*" *So afraid of Mommy. She might take her love away if I don't dance like her puppet.* **Bullshit!** *You never loved me, anyway. I've stunted and denied my life for you, and* **you didn't even care, you bitch!**

I have a word for you, Mother. The word for you is **No!** *You want me to say,* "*Yes, Mommy, yes. I'll be your baby. Yes, I'll eat your garbage. Yes, I'll love you. Yes, I'll be a nothing for you.*" *Well, I don't say 'Yes' anymore, Mommy. I say* **No!!** **No, No, No, No, No,** *from now on,* **No!** *Never again will I eat your shit. Go to hell, Mommy. From now on I'm me!*

Afterward I am completely dazed. I don't know exactly where I have been. Mostly I am aware of my own feelings, my vigorous movement with the pillow (I have never beaten anything so hard), of the cries and screams that well up from deep inside, my sense of loss and outrage, and pain, and anger. I expected to cry, but I didn't. I cried out. *When I open my eyes I feel weak, and the room looks unreal to me. It is like coming to after an operation—disorientation about time and place. My body is tired. I felt lightheaded this morning when I woke up. I had only six hours of sleep and usually*

*feel kind of rocky after that, but instead I feel
good—rested, light. I'm not sure what has happened
to me. I hope it is the beginning of a new way to
be, a new freedom from my mother.*

After Mother's bitch session most people feel remarkably
similar: a mixture of exhaustion, cleanliness, and relief. While
they are purged of their anger toward mother, (and no one is
allowed to continue in the Process until they are), they are
not finished with her. For the moment they are instructed
to leave mother's negative crud piled in a corner of the sanctuary. Later, father's negativity will be added to the compost
heap, to be used for recycling in the final session.

I wonder how you are feeling about *your* mother now?

CHAPTER VII

"EVERYONE IS GUILTY AND NO ONE IS TO BLAME!

Mother. *Mutter. Mere. Madre.* In any language or culture the word calls forth powerful images. Close your eyes for a moment and permit yourself to free associate with the word "mother."

What have you come up with? A long list of motherly attributes? Some physical characteristics of mothers, perhaps? Possibly you relived a few childhood scenes.

If you are like most people, you associate "mother" with an adult woman. We usually picture mothers as grown and mature, at least physically. While our normal visualization of mother is accurate, seeing her only as an adult blinds us to a crucial truth: Mother was a *child once* herself. While everyone "knows" their mother was once a child, the full meaning of this fact has little impact on most of us. Instead, we tend to feel and think about mother as the grown woman we looked up to: larger, stronger, older, more knowing, supposedly more loving than we were and one with especially endowed powers. From our childhood space of dependency, mother was our rock, our goddess: with little or no questioning we took for granted her supreme authority and "wisdom." Our later intellectual understanding was that mother was not always an ideal model. We then spend years blaming mother for our emotional problems. Seldom do we experience deeply and emotionally the agonizing negative love tragedy mother suffered as a child. In the next stage of the Process we remedy this *critical deficiency* in our perception of her.

We now defend and learn to emotionally exonerate her of blame. This state of relaxed openness, created by the exhilerated feeling of autonomy resulting from the bitch session, makes possible the abrupt and thorough shift from the negativity of mother's prosecution to the positivity of her defense. In this step of the process mother is seen and experienced not as the adult she was, but as the child she was. To simply say, "Oh, yes, I know she had it tough as a kid," without experiencing it fully and deeply is an intellectual headtrip and has no lasting positive effect.

The truth of the negative love syndrome is that *everyone is guilty and no one is to blame*. True, we found her guilty during the prosecution stage, but *she is not to blame*. She programmed you to be the way you are and the irrefutable fact is that her parents programmed her to be the way she was and is.

In the Defense of Mother, you have an opportunity to go beyond blaming to understanding. There are five steps in learning to love. The first is to understand *without condemnation*. The second step is to learn compassion, which the dictionary defines as "profound feeling for the misfortune of others and a desire to aid them" or "sorrow for another's plight or predicament accompanied by a strong desire to alleviate the pain or remove its cause." (The final three steps are taken in Closure, described in Chapter 12.)

Who then was this woman, your mother? What was she all about? You may have thought you knew her well, but did you? What were mother's parents (your grandparents) really like? Forget the white-haired folks with bifocals you may remember fondly from your childhood. Consider instead the young parents they were in their twenties and thirties. What was it like for mother to have been the child of your grandparents? (All the rude questions we asked about your love life, sex life, childhood with mother, and so forth, are relevant to mother as well as to you.) Whatever it was like, her family experience made your mother the child she was, the woman and wife she became, and the mother you knew. In the Prosecution stage everyone sees himself as the victim of mother the bitch. In the Defense stage we learn to see mother as the victim of *her* bitch mother and bastard father.

The metaphor of two sides of a coin helps make the point that prosecuting mother for her sins of omission and commission is one-sided. The other side of the coin is that if you are thirty years old and your mother is sixty, she has endured the affliction of unloveability twice as many years as you have and she deserves twice as much compassion as you do. You can still avoid living out the remainder of your life in negative love, but chances are your mother was or is beyond this hope.

No, it is never too late to learn to love. The oldest person to go through the Process so far is a seventy-four-year-old woman who found freedom through a loving divorce from her long-dead parents. She finally learned to love first herself, then her children, and grandchildren.

If your mother is already dead, how much more poignant is her love tragedy. After all those years of living in the wasteland of no real love, she never made it. She went to her grave with her own frightened lonely hurt little child trapped inside.

The explanation of mother's tragic lack of love in life is largely the same as yours: No one taught her to love during her formative childhood years. She could not teach you what she herself never learned. She contracted the disease of negative love from her mother and father just as you did from your parents—who got it from their parents, who got it from their parents, who got it from *their* parents, and so on back in time and space to the first men and women. Yes, negative love is the world's most devastating emotional disease because it is insidiously "passed on from generation to generation in all peoples and families."

By overthrowing the force of negative love, you can absolve mother for *her* karma for the negativities and unloveability she *helplessly* inflicted on you. In so doing you take a great step forward in your own karma* progression. The *worst* of all the karmic debts we take upon ourselves in this lifetime is the perpetuation of negative love patterns. Cleaning them away and permitting our innate loving positivity to surface is the way to spiritual progression and enlightenment.

While the chain of negative love reaches endlessly backward in time, it does *not have to continue* forward into the future. Yours is the link that can be broken.

---

*Karma is the testing which individuals (and groups) impose upon themselves by their actions, both positive and negative; the force or effect these accumulated actions have on our lives.

The psychic technology of mind revelations is used extensively in the Defense of Mother. In the first stage of the defense a dialogue takes place between the client's negative emotional child at age thirteen (or whenever puberty occurred) and mother's negative emotional child at about the same age. The conversation between the two children, in which mother's child provides answers to important questions about her childhood, produces a compassionate understanding of the emotional deprivation she experienced. What the child within mother describes to the client is often quite similar to his own trauma, making it possible for the two to empathize with one another. The dialogue, like the remainder of the Defense of Mother, is *not* a fantasy or guided imagery. It is a mind revelation employing natural sensory perception abilities in order to receive and tune into the emotional experiences of mother's past. Strange as it may seem, this mind revelation always produces deep level compassion. No one has yet failed to experience this. When clients check out the validity of information obtained they always discover that the essence is accurate.

The next step after the dialogue is a monologue in which mother's psychic Trinity, with the knowledge gleaned from the dialogue, dictates to her son or daughter her negative emotional autobiography with *her* mother and father. As she recounts her own childhood programming, the client is shocked to discover that mother's childhood was similar in its loneliness, frustration, and lack of parental warmth and love. In the monologue mother gives a year-by-year account of how she, like her son or daughter, grew up with manipulation, deceit, and a lack of consistent love. Mother learned her negativity the same way the client did, from her Mama and Papa.

The dialogue, followed by the monologue, prepares the way for the Trial-log, which integrates mother's defense. It is the log of a trial with three participants:

1. The client's negative emotional child at age thirteen,

2. Mother's adult Trinity at age she was when the client was thirteen,

3. The client's perfect spiritual self, who acts as judge-moderator.

In the Trial-log the client's negative emotional child has a final opportunity to purge itself of any residual anger and resentment toward mother. It begins like a second bitch session. But this time mother, with her newly acquired knowledge of her childhood programming, uses her adult intellect to defend herself against the accustations. The client's vengeful child may want to continue to gripe and complain over the wrongs mother did, instead of developing his understanding with no condemnation. Should this happen, the client's spiritual self is present to intervene and make sure his child self is willing to experience the other side of mother, the side that was crippled emotionally in her childhood and left powerless to do other than she did. During the Trial-Log the client's spiritual self influences him to give up blaming mother and replace the vengeance with deep compassionate understanding.

After this three-step mind revelation process is successfully completed it is possible to let go of negativity, hostility, bitching, and anger at mother while moving closer to learning to love her and yourself. Then to consolidate the Defense of Mother, a mind revelation, Mother's Compassion Scene, is experienced. In this procedure the client sees, and then emotionally experiences, mother's death as though it were happening. He experiences it as real, whether she is presently alive or deceased. Watching mother going to her grave, actually being lowered into the ground with her unloved negative emotional child still trapped within her, evokes heartfelt sadness and empathy. The client sheds compassionate tears for her wasted life as an unloved woman, wife, and mother for her tragedy duplicated and exceeded his own. Anger and resentment are totally dissipated.

Reading about the experience of Mother's Defense is tame in comparison to living it as Laura, Nancy, and Chris did. Each of them lived through a powerful, unsettling, but ultimately life-restoring transformation in their Defense of Mother. The emotional impact of the three steps of the defense is cumulative, but the information itself is much the same. For the sake of brevity, therefore, only one segment from each defense is given: (1) Laura's dialogue with her mother's thirteen-year-old negative emotional child, (2) Chris's monologue, in which his mother dictates her negative emotional autobiography with her mother and father, and (3) Nancy's Trial-log of her negative emotional child, her mother's adult Trinity, with Nancy's spiritual self as judge-moderator. Chris's description of Mother's Compassion Scene, which concludes the chapter, is typical of the experience of most clients.

LAURA'S DIALOGUE WITH MOTHER

In this discussion with her mother's child at puberty, Laura experiences at first-hand the origin of mother's negative traits—the traits that have caused them both so much suffering. Her mother, Alice, had been programmed by her parents to be unloving, a goody-goody, falsely cheerful, obsessed with appearances and hundreds of other negative traits to which Laura responded with either adoption or rebellion. Within these excerpts of her dialogue, you will see how Laura came to understand how her mother, too, was victimized by negative love.

After a mind revelation to prepare her, Laura begins:

> *My mother appears in my sanctuary. My guide asks Mother's intellect and mine to observe and learn but not to interfere. Now it is just my negative emotional child at puberty confronting my mother's emotional child at the same age.*
>
> Laura: *Hello, little girl who grew up to be my mother. How was it with you and your parents?*
>
> Alice: *Most of my childhood was unhappy. When I was just a little baby, my father died. (We were happier until then. Mother said he was always cheerful and smiling.) He had a heart attack during the night, and my mother didn't know what to do for him. She didn't understand how sick he was, and in the morning he was dead. All her life after that she felt she had killed him, and she never got over it.*

Laura: *That must have been terrible!*

Alice: *It was very sad for all of us. My mother and my aunts and my big brother cried, and I cried, too. After that I never knew what it was to have a father. I always longed for a father. I would have liked to sit on my Daddy's lap and have him hold me the way I saw some of my friend's fathers do.*

Laura: *That does sound lonely.*

Alice: *My mother was always sad after my father died, though she pretended to feel all right in front of outsiders. I tried to comfort her as best I could, but I just felt helpless because I couldn't. We were very poor, too. My mother didn't know how to support us, and she was always worried about food and clothing.*

Laura: *So you were afraid and worried and feeling helpless when you were a little girl. And you were sad because your mother was sad, but that didn't make her feel any better.*

Alice: *Sometimes I felt that my mother would have been better off if I hadn't been born. I felt guilty for being around, for being another mouth to feed.*

Laura: *Didn't that make you feel resentful? Did you sometimes hate your mother for making you feel unwanted?*

Alice: *I'm ashamed to admit that, but it's true. Sometimes I secretely hated my mother for making me feel so wretched. But then I tried even harder to* act *happy around her so that I'd make up for being angry at her. Most of all I resented the way she preferred my brother John to me. He was her first baby, and she loved him in a way she never loved me. She felt that I was just another ignorant female like her who didn't know how to save her husband's life or earn a living for her children. She really despised herself for being a woman, and so she despised me for being a woman, too.*

Laura: *I'm beginning to see why you were so uncaring and cold to me. You never were treated with love yourself.*

Alice: *I didn't know how to be warm and affectionate. I never learned that from my only parent. I never felt OK inside, or worthy or happy. I decided I wouldn't be sad like my mother. I'd be like my daddy had been. So I learned to smile all the time and pretend that everything was all right. It never felt right inside. But I thought if I didn't upset mother, maybe she would love me.*

Laura: *I'm beginning to see where you got so much of your negativity. But how about being so manipulative? You tried to make me into a puppet.*

Alice: *I had to learn how to manipulate people because there wasn't any other way of getting what I wanted. I knew nobody loved me enough to give me anything, so I had to get it some other way. My mother manipulated John and me with her cold silences, her sad looks, and her criticism. I decided never to do that, but I guess I ended up doing it, anyway. I wanted so many things I couldn't have when I was a little child. Even new, warm underwear would have been a treat. So I thought when I grew up and became a mother I would give my children lots of things, birthday parties, Christmas gifts, and pretty clothes, and then they would always love me.*

Laura: *You learned how to act loving even if you didn't feel it.*

Alice: *Yes, when I grew up I did what I thought mommies ought to do: kiss the baby and hold it when company came. I thought a clean, well-dressed baby was a loved baby. I became a Pollyanna, pretending that everything was all right because that was the way I thought I could get my mother to love me. I was a good little girl for my mother. I swept and washed dishes and sewed. I walked on tiptoes around her. I still am a very good girl even though I'm almost grown up now. I try to do whatever my mother wants, and in many ways I am just like her, but it doesn't help. It seems as if all my life she is saying to me, "I'll love you if you're good, or quiet, or helpful, or if you comfort me." But she never loved me for me.*

At the end of much more discussion, Laura was able to say,

> *I understand your life now. I really can't condemn you. You just didn't have much choice. You endured as much pain as I. How terrible!*

During and after this dialogue Laura understood with no condemnation why her mother treated her as she did. She had no doubt she was communicating with the child who grew up to become her mother. Experience has proven that mind revelations do not lie. She experienced the reality of this mind revelation and, like hundreds of others before her, gleaned new information about her mother's childhood which she was able to subsequently verify. The emotional essence of the dialogue is always true. Poor mother was negatively programmed by the grandparents and unwittingly passed it along to her children.

Once the facts of mother's negative love programming and emotional anguish are clear, the second step is to produce the monologue. Chris, having completed his dialogue with his mother, understands the forces that shaped her. His mother's psychic Trinity dictates her emotional autobiography, while he listens. Again, the following portrays *only* the *highlights* of mother's story.

CHRIS'S MOTHER'S MONOLOGUE

> *Superficially my childhood was rich, and I should have been thought to have everything—position, status, stable parents, intelligence, good looks. Actually, most of my life was hell. My dad was the son of poor parents and worked his way through medical school, working twenty hours a day much of the time. My mother was beautiful and married him for his position-to-be. They had me earlier than they were ready, while he was still struggling to start a practice. Mother was a social climber in a covert way, and Dad was aloof and demanding of himself. Mother was demanding of everyone. So I was born into their conflicts and frustrations.*

Mother's family was more socially acceptable than Dad's, and when he hid out in his office behind his medical journals, she turned her sharp tongue and ambitious eyes on me. I was her first born, looked like her and was expected to be like her.

People used to say how gracious Mother was, but I don't think so. She was as nasty as anybody, just slier about it. She worried about the impression I made, so I had to dress just so, even curtsy. I had to keep quiet and out of Dad's way when he had patients coming. Dad let Mom rule the house. I was often ashamed by his kowtowing to her. Men weren't supposed to be like that. But he was, and people outside the family never saw it. I don't know whether it was more Dad or Mom, but they used his profession to not relate to me. I might as well have been a robot myself or a puppet. Except I got to take it out on my sisters. Sister Lucy got her attention by being bad, cranky, loud, obnoxious. I had to try to get my love by conforming, being a goody-goody. I didn't have much chance with Mother's manipulating and rock-hard authoritarianism and Dad's moralistic withdrawal. They both spent lots of time invalidating me. Sometimes Mother pretended to listen, but she only used my feelings against me, demanding, shaming me, putting me down.

Things were especially bad when my next sister, Mary, was born. Mom said she was difficult, but she forced me to take responsibility for her. It wasn't till later that I wondered if she was by a different father, but of course that was not to be talked about. Dad was so shut off from talking with me, and maybe from his own feelings, that I still don't know if he really wanted a boy. But I was always somehow aware that he was not with me. He let my mother raise me, and though he seemed to like the attention of us females, he never was close.

They couldn't even let me seek love elsewhere without constant warning about how others weren't *as good as we were. God, I was lonely! When I wasn't lonely, I was angry and fearfully not showing it—angry at Dad for not taking time to listen to me, or for letting that controlling bitch mother shut me out. He had his work; I didn't have anything.*

I wish Mother had had the humanity really to let go, hug me, touch me, be loving. But no, she was cold, aristocratic, aloof, and so smart that anything I tried to do to get attention either was doing her thing, not being myself, being a traitor to my own needs, or it backfired and brought angry criticism, with devastating looks or words. My parents gave credit for positive qualities only if they were the ones they decided on. I wanted credit for being me, their little girl.

Two of a kind they were: perfectionists, aloof, demanding, suppressed, unaffectionate, with duty before pleasure and adults before children. Yes, Chris, I guess you could call me the lonely, poor little rich girl!

After hearing his mother's childhood history, Chris is left with no doubt where, how, and why she became a Zombie who then programmed him to be a Zombie just like her. As he emotionally experiences how his mother adopted her negative traits, he begins to understand her without condemning her. He also learns there is no emotional need to cling to his false Zombie exterior and the other negative patterns that were not really hers any more than they are his.

After her own dialogue and monologue with mother, Nancy, too, is close to reaching the needed understanding with no condemnation of mother. It remains for Nancy to clean out the last remnants of anger and resentment by giving her negative emotional child permission for a final opportunity to speak out and have a second day in court. From time to time her spiritual self intervenes to help her accept the ultimate truth: *Everyone is guilty, and no one is to blame.*

NANCY'S TRIAL-LOG WITH MOTHER

My child self, my spiritual self, and my mother's adult living mind spirit (newly aware) are in my sanctuary. My child is permitted and encouraged to vent any residual bitchiness, my spiritual self with awareness has the authority to preside, and Mother is imbued with the desire to explain and defend herself based solely on her new understanding of her childhood.

Nancy's Child: *I still hate you! I'm miserable, and it's all your fault.*

Adult Mother: *Yes, I can see that now. I was trying so hard to be a good mother, and actually I've been teaching you all the unhappiness and disappointment in life I learned from my own parents.*

Nancy's Child: *What good does it do me if you see it now? You should have seen what you were doing earlier. What right did you have to go around being so fucking sorry for yourself and teaching me self-pity?*

Adult Mother: *I felt sorry for myself, as my mother felt sorry for herself. I really believed that I was nothing if my man left me. That's how my mother felt, and I see now that I couldn't outdo her. I still wanted her love when I should have been mothering you.*

Nancy's Child: *Yah! You were nothing either way. I don't blame Dad for leaving you. You were self-righteous, critical, and a bad-tempered drag, anyway!*

Spiritual Self: *Easy there, child. You know now how she got that way. In your talk with her thirteen-year-old you found out what her childhood was like.*

Nancy's Child: *But all you ever did was play mother. Big dramatic scenes. Never there when I really needed you. Running me down while expecting me to build you up. Confused! Insecure! Afraid of other people! Damn you for all that, anyhow! You taught it to me.*

Adult Mother: *Again, like my mother. She didn't believe she was as good as my father, or even as his sister. She felt put down by them both. But when he obviously preferred other women, the only hold she had on him, the only position she had in life, that of wife, came crashing down. I know now that through negative love I became just like her.*

Nancy's Child: *And all that phony pretense you laid on me. The phony smiles, the lack of self-love. That's the worst! You had no real self, no self-respect, only that empty pride. You didn't love yourself!*

Adult Mother: *I had no way of learning. My parents had no self-love, and my position as the third and unwanted girl, Henry coming along after me and being the son they wanted, left me with no right even to exist. I felt that I was somehow just tolerated because I was there, not because I had a right to be there.*

Nancy's Child: *I won't feel sorry for you! You were a rotten, uncaring mother!*

Spiritual Self: *No one is asking you to feel sorry for her, child. Only to listen and to understand.*

Adult Mother: *What my mother gave me was pseudo-love. I always felt that she was playing at being grown-up. She had no confidence in herself. The only way she got what she wanted was by getting my father or my aunt, and later her children, to give it to her.*

Nancy's Child: *But all that repressed anger of yours and the wild outbursts of temper—you laid those on me. I walked on eggshells around you, you Goddamned volcano. I never knew when you'd blow off!*

Adult Mother: *My father was always very distant with us as children and maintained his position as head of the house by keeping us in fear of him. We were too much in awe of him to treat him with anything but utmost respect openly. But he was a liar and a phony, and he resented us. We all knew he had a terrible temper and we were all afraid of arousing him. He was terribly critical of us all, while he was self-righteous about his own behavior. He felt himself superior to other people, and especially to my mother, but inside he was weak and phony. Don't you see that I adopted all that through negative love?*

Nancy's Child: *I guess I do see. But the suffering? How did you learn to let yourself suffer that way, to have no self-caring?*

Adult Mother: *Starting when I was about nine, and for several years after that, my father had a mistress. We weren't supposed to know, but everybody did. My mother was by turns hysterical and grief stricken. I heard my older sisters talking about it and imagined that my mother would become like my aunt, unwanted and without a man to support her, and I worried terribly about what would become of us all. Actually, my father did not desert us totally and continued to support us, but my mother suffered terribly over his neglect during those years.*

Nancy's Child: *You actually had the same kind of father I did!*

Adult Mother: *Yes, I married a man who was just like my father. My father had wanted to be a poet but had to work in an office all his life to support his four children. He'd fallen in love with my mother and married her, but later he felt trapped by her and resented her.*

Nancy's Child: *So you learned resentment that way, I see. But where did you get your authoritarianism and anger?*

Adult Mother: *From my father. He ruled us by putting us all down and insisting on being the only important person there.*

Nancy's Child: *So you had no way to learn to be a woman and to enjoy sex?*

Adult Mother: *No one told me about sex, or that it was all right to have a body, when I was a child. I just learned there was something frightening and bad about relations between men and women.*

(My child self puts her hand quietly on mother's shoulder and shakes her head sadly.)
  Nancy's Child: *I really do see, Mother. (She has tears in her eyes.) Poor Mother. You were caught in this negative love trap just as I was.*

As the Trial-log closes, Nancy compassionately under-stands that mother could not help herself any more than Nancy could. Nancy has again accused mother of teaching her the traits that devastated her life, as she did in the bitch session, but this time is ready to hear her mother's defense. Mother's answers to her questions, fully understood and heard by Nancy's Trinity, enable her to finally relinquish her anger toward mother, leaving a space for positive emotions to emerge. The removal of the residual anger, bringing compas-sion in its place, differs completely from simple Baygull for-giveness or Zombie denial of the anger.
  Laura, Chris and Nancy were each moved to tears by their dialogue, Mother's Negative Emotional Autobiography, and Trial-log. But this level of compassion, although genuine, is not enough to wash away completely the agony of the years of repressed hostility. Each of them must then live through a dramatic compassion scene for their mother, seeing her going to her grave with her negative emotional child still within, never having a chance to grow up and become a whole, truly loving human being. This then brings them to the deepest level of human compassion.

A CONDENSED VERSION OF
CHRIS'S COMPASSION SCENE FOR MOTHER

I get home and my daughter tells me my mother has been killed in a traffic accident. I feel a sudden wrenching shock. I call my wife to come home and stay with the kids. I drive to the hospital. At the hospital I'm shown a gurney with a body covered by a sheet. Lifting the sheet, I see it's my mother—dead! I am stunned and feel sick. I ask to be alone with her for a few minutes. Sitting next to her body, I take her cold hand in mine and think of the promises I've made to spend more time to get to know her. I think especially of this process, which is giving me an opportunity to change so I can actually express love for her. At the funeral home the next day I look inside her with psychic x-ray vision and see her child, scared, hurt, never fulfilled. I gently place a single red rose on her breast and see the little hands of her pathetic negative child reaching to clutch it. (Tears.) She never became a woman, never had a chance really to be a mother to me or anyone else. Now I'll never get to know her. She'll never really know me, her only son. (More tears.)

Later, at the graveside, I look at her coffin and feel the heavy weight of sadness for that unloved, unloving, never-grown child in her. She had such an empty seventy-four years. I was such a stingy, insensitive, scared son. (Cried some more, on and off, through much of this typing.) Oh, Mother, you had seventy-four (it probably seemed like 174) years! I've had forty-six with you, and we've never really been able to love each other. (Sobbing.) Why did you have to die just when that damn negative love chain was being broken, when I might have learned to love you? We never even knew each other. We had so much in common and so little love.

Don't die yet. I will be free! I will learn to love! I'll become a loving son and fulfill you even though you couldn't fulfill me. Mother, don't be dead! (More sobbing.)

With these words of sadness and compassion, Chris ended his work with mother for the moment. He had not yet learned to love her, but he had freed himself of his deeply repressed anger. She was no longer a bitch, and he was no longer a Zombie. It was wonderful to see his facial expressions and body. His whole being had come alive.

The changes in the others at this time were equally dramatic. Nancy became softer and more approachable to other people. Laura lost her Baygull sweetness and replaced it with a more straightforward demeanor. She continued to smile, but not compulsively. All of them were far more real than ever before in their lives. They were on their way to discovering self-love.

The Defense of Mother proves that negative love is like a locked cage, and intellect is not the key. No amount of intellectual "knowing" or head tripping about her childhood experiences can evoke true compassion for her. To give up blaming her is not just an intellectual decision but a deeply felt emotional commitment. You must experience her life, or "walk a mile in her shoes," to paraphrase an American Indian saying, to find real compassion for her.

Once you have experienced mother as an unloved little girl, your perspective takes an about-face. The Bitch is no more. In her place is a child of the Godhead, just like you and everyone else. She is inadvertently guilty, but not to blame, for your childhood misery. When you can feel for mother as a real person victimized by negative love, you are closer to becoming an autonomous, loving human being.

CHAPTER VIII

"GO TO HELL, DADDY!"

We have rightfully exonerated Mother. The next phase of the Process is to examine father's overt and covert contributions to your negative love problems.

Father's marital failure to fulfill your mother lies at the center of the entire constellation of family problems you knew as a child. The traits such as hostility, abandonment, withdrawal, the pseudo-love and dishonest communication, etc.—however unlovingness was expressed in your home— your father's failure as a husband and a father was a crucial source. If he was not a strong central figure in the family, exuding confidence, emotional stability, and a flow of consistent warmth and love, everyone suffered, particularly your mother. If she was bitter and unloving, look to your father. He is the one most guilty for the lack of a loving atmosphere in the home. Having a husband she cannot relate to in love and respect is the ultimate heartbreak and frustration for a woman. Poor mother may have been a bitch, but father was a real bastard.

In the Process most people have less difficulty seeing father as the culprit. Overcoming the resistance against full awareness of mother during her Prosecution prepares the way to do the same during father's Prosecution. Also, father, more often than mother, is the villain in the childhood recollections. He was usually the one who wielded the power in the home, and also the most distant. Fathers have traditionally been expected to provide for their families and be the rock of security on which the family depends. Mothers have been expected to be soft, warm and not as strong as men. When the "rock" is not in evidence—when father is not "there" for his children—the end result is pent-up resentment, bitterness, rage, and loveless insecurity. Father's failure to be a father is a major source of neurotic self-hate.

The Prosecution and Defense of Father is like that of mother in almost all respects. To be free of father's negative influence, you must first recognize how his negative traits were expressed by re-living your childhood experiences with him, putting full awareness and focus on his negativity and how it's contributed to your adult problems. As the important first step, writing the Negative Emotional Autobiography with Father prepares you for the hostile space needed for the bitch session. As with mother, the full fury of the anger and resentment toward father must be experienced and released in order to be free of his negative influence.

Directing attention to father's negative traits incites the covert anger that lies dormant. Yet his positive traits, like those of mother, are also a source of emotional difficulty and must not be *overlooked*. The positive traits that cause difficulty are the only ones against which an angry child will rebel to gain revenge and *negative attention*. If father gets things done promptly, for example, the negative emotional child may show his angry face to father through procrastination. The real life consequences of procrastination (lost friends, lost time, lost income) will be added to the conflict. The client already suffers. The conflict itself stems from feeling two powerful, contradictory emotions simultaneously: anger and guilt. Anger, of course, stems from feeling unloved, and the guilt is derived by rejecting the adoption of father's positive traits. "You don't love me, so I'll show you. I won't love you," says the rebellious negative emotional child.

As they did with mother, clients prepare to bitch at father by reviewing the list of his negative traits, moods, and admonitions, both silent and overt. They are shocked to discover that they are the bastard father all over again by adopting his negative traits as their own. Even though they have already experienced this irrefutable truth with mother, people are always amazed and surprised to see how like their (negative) fathers they really are. Their anguish is further complicated because the few positive traits of father's are often directly opposite to mother's negative traits, while the few positive traits of mother's are offset by the opposite negative traits in father. If mother rarely got things done on schedule, and father always did, their child will be inconsistent in his behavior. "Damned if you do, and damned if you don't" describes the double bind exactly.

Tallying father's negative traits and honestly deciding how you responded to them (adoption or rebellion) has the same enraging effect as it did with mother. And as before a mere intellectual understanding will not do. The long suppressed anger must be vented.

What kind of father did you have? How was his relationship with mother during your embryo period? How did father feel about mother during pregnancy? Did he look forward to your addition to the family? Or were you a surprise and a burden, unwanted even before you were born?

Are you the sex your father wanted you to be? Or did you disappoint him? If you were the son he wanted, did he treat you as his heir apparent, expecting you to make your life the fulfillment of all the ambitions he never achieved? Or was he envious of you, teaching you never to be better at anything than he was? Did he give you the admonition, "Don't outdo me"? Even now, do you see your strengths and weaknesses only by comparing yourself with him? Did he tell you that you will never amount to anything or that you are no good?

Perhaps you were a daughter instead of the son he wanted. How did he deal with your femaleness? Did he ignore you, teaching you that only men counted? Or did he cover his negative feelings toward you, his daughter, by offering you pseudo-love? What did Daddy's model of manhood teach you about men? That men are cold and distant? Or perhaps Daddy's weakness and immaturity taught you that men are overgrown babies needing constant attention? Either way, he cheated you of your right to see and experience a model of properly developed manhood.

When you were an infant, did father only play with you when he felt like it? Or was he aware of your need for his loving attention at all times? Did he arrange his life to be able to meet your need? Or did he put his own needs ahead of yours? If he played with you when you were happy, did he also attend to you when you were wet, or sick, or otherwise less than beautiful? Or was he a fair-weather father, only interested in you when you didn't ask anything in return?

Later, when you were a toddler, did he give you time and attention when you needed it? Or did he brush you off with a pat on the head or perhaps with an angry rebuke for intruding on him? If he had *loved to love* he would have spent a great deal of time with you in your childhood. Had he wanted to, he could have received more fulfillment and positive energy by giving his love to you and receiving love from you than by copping out, napping or hiding behind newspapers. Instead of giving a loving, consistent flow of communication, were there constant barrages of hostile demands? When did Daddy hold you in his arms and how often did he tell you that he loved you? (If he did?)

Did father share with mother in your upbringing? Or did he let her decide how you were to be cared for? Was he just a meal ticket and policeman, while providing no warmth or direction to your childhood? Was father *there* but *"not there"* for you?

Your attitudes toward women come directly from the way your father related to your mother. What was your father's attitude toward your mother? Did he respect and admire her? Was she his model of womanhood? Or did he run her down to build himself up, thus teaching you not to respect women, as well as to become a put-down artist? Or did he put your mother on a pedestal, teaching you that women are everything and men are nothing, so that you learned how to grovel at women's feet? When he came home after work (assuming that he *did* come home) did he take her in his arms and caress her tenderly making her feel cared for, wanted, and loved? Or did he drag himself through the door, give her a perfunctory nod or a dutiful peck on the cheek, and retreat to the television or behind a magazine? If so, he is the culprit responsible for your mother becoming the disappointed, angry, castrating wife and woman you knew. His distance, non-involvement, and indifference drained her of emotional goodness and aggravated her negativity. It was father's responsibility to melt mother's icy demeanor.

Father's love should enfold mother and the children if a loving home life is to thrive. When father came home, did he kiss mother and ignore you? Did you feel rejected and left out? Did you say to yourself something like, "OK for you,

Daddy. If you won't love me too, I won't love you"? If so, he's the one who is responsible for your continuing to feel left out and rejected by others or to *reject others before they reject you.* Both patterns of unfulfillment come from father's stupidity in not including you in the family love circle.

How did father wield his power as head of the house? Was he a tyrant, angrily insisting that things be his way or else? Did everyone have to arrange their lives to suit him? Did he insist on silence at the dinner table, thus stifling any loving communication during these moments the family was together? Was your mother little more than his servant and you his "go-for"? Did he teach you to be sullenly compliant while secretly resentful? Much of your attitude toward men in authority is derived from the way you saw father exercise his power over you and your mother.

Or was father a weakling who gave in to everyone? When mother disagreed with him did he just nod and say, "Yes, dear. Whatever you say, dear"? Did father teach you to avoid "making waves" so that even today you dare not disagree openly with anyone and assert yourself?

Did your father allow your mother to emasculate him? If so, he taught you to see men as weaklings dominated by women. If she ran the house and everyone in it, it's his fault for not being the loving adult male every household needs, to be complete. If he cannot stand up to her, how will she respect and love his manhood? Every married woman, whether she helps support the family financially or not, needs to know that the man she has thrown her lot in with can be counted on to "be there" emotionally for her. She must trust his strength, and have her essence be complemented by his. She also needs to feel accepted by him as an equal, rather than dismissed as an exploited inferior. For love, warmth, and emotional goodness to exist and grow, husband and wife must be mates on an equal basis.

How inconsistent was his love and warmth for you and your brothers and sisters? Did you feel tolerated by him, sensing that he often wished you weren't around? Were you just a mouth to feed? Did he praise your achievements as well as correct your errors? Or did you get mostly negative attention from him, thus learning that the way to get him to notice you was to get in trouble? Are you still goofing off today, at home and at work, to continue to get father's negative attention? If so, the unhappy consequence of this horrible pattern can be laid at the feet of father, the bastard.

Did your father teach you to get along well with your brothers and sisters? To love them? Or did he make you compete for his love, thus teaching you resentment, jealousy, and sibling rivalry? Father should have played an important role in presenting you to the older children in the family in order to avoid sibling rivalry (as described in Chapter 5).

What kind of discipline did father use? The cast-iron fist, the limp wrist, or the firm, but loving hand? Did he use punishment fairly as a means to help you learn? Or did he use it cruelly? Was he so wrapped up in his own concerns that he didn't bother to teach you right from wrong? If your father had been a loving man, he would have disciplined you with love.

When your father did spend time with you, what did you do together? Who decided how you would spend the time? Did you do only the things he wanted to do? Or did you do things he thought were "good for you"? Or was he so guilty over his failure to really love you that he always let you do whatever you wanted? A loving father is flexible, neither controlling his children totally nor leaving them without guidance.

If your father had money, was he generous with it? Did he teach you to see money as a means of providing necessities and a few luxuries? Or did he use money to buy you off with presents that were really bribes and guilt offerings? Did he give you a regular allowance and teach you to manage money? Or stifling your humiliation, did you have to beg for money? As you grew old enough to understand, did he inform you of the family's financial affairs? Or did he keep you in the dark so that you would never be able to question his decisions or learn to make your own?

If the family was well-off, did he "buy" household help who saw to your daily upbringing, thus relieving him of any responsibility? If so, he was your father in a biological sense only, a man who was there but not there, a phantom father.

What about when you gave him gifts on special days? Did he appreciate your thoughtfulness? Or was he unresponsive to your gifts, leaving you with the feeling that nothing you could give him would please him? Or whatever you did for him wasn't good enough? Did your father teach you to hate him by refusing your gifts as tokens of your love?

What were your father's reactions when you brought your report card home? Was he indifferent to your grades? Or did he have expectations that were impossible to meet? Did he insist that only straight A's were good enough for *his* child? Or did he send you the message that you were stupid, thus ensuring that you would never develop your full ability? Did he punish you for low marks while ignoring you when you did well? Or could he care less? If you are still getting more negative than positive attention, you can look to your bastard father as the cause.

Was father a Don Juan who had to make it with all the women in sight in order to prove his masculinity? If so, he neglected his family and their need for his love.

What kind of worker was father? Did he work compulsively from early morning until late at night? If so, you hardly ever saw him except when he was too tired to give you needed loving attention? Or was he shiftless and unrealiable so that you were in constant fear of financial insecurity? Was his life a healthy mixture of work and leisure? If not, he again failed you. A child needs a model of a balanced life if he is to create one for himself.

Did your father know the difference between being a father and being a friend? Did he try to buddy up to you and be your pal to impress you with what a "great guy" he was? Companionship is great, but children need a loving adult father, not an aging playmate.

Did your father demand, however subtly, that you live up to his expectations of you? Did he insist that you go to college or graduate school, or perhaps enter a particular profession, in order to fulfill his frustrated ambitions of thirty years ago? Did he want you to be what he never had the time, money, or opportunity to become? Were you forced into a hated career you didn't want? Others have spent their lives working far below their potential because they rebelled against their father's oppressive manipulations and demands for achievement.

Did your father have a sense of humor? How much and how often did he laugh, and what kind of laughter was it? Jolly? Sarcastic? Mocking? Phony? Was he able to laugh at himself as well as at others? Or was he a sour-puss who thought humor was silly and childish? A humorless father is a terrible curse. If your father never laughed with you, he destroyed much of your natural capacity for fun and pleasure.

How did father fulfill his responsibility for your sexual education? Did he take the time to prepare you for sexual adulthood? Did he help you understand the meaning of your first menstrual period or your first ejaculation? How did he greet your puberty—the all-important time of your becoming a biological adult. Did he make you feel like a man or a woman?

Have you found what he told you about sex to be true and helpful, or did he pass along misinformation and prejudices from his childhood? What would it be like to live in a world filled with men who are sexually like your father?

Did father die in your early childhood? If so, he deserted you, for death is desertion. It is necessary to prosecute dead fathers because there are still negative traits one adopts through hearsay or having actually experienced them during the pre-natal period and early childhood. If mother never remarried, then father's desertion in death left you without a father or a father image. If father in reality deserted and abandoned you, then he is even more guilty of creating your rejection pattern that says, "I'm not good enough to be loved by father," or "I am not worthy of a man's love."

If mother did remarry, what was your stepfather like? Your stepfather is then the father surrogate, and all the rude questions about father apply to him as well.

As with mother, father's *acts of omission* are as important as his acts of commission. Were there areas of father-child life about which he said or did nothing? Whatever he ignored or overlooked has left a gaping hole in your development as a complete adult. What kind of father did *you* have?

If you have not already done so, now is the time to take father off his pedestal. Whether you have been aware of it or not, he is responsible for most of your life problems. Your father's many failings as a man, husband, and father are a major source of your deepest anxieties, conflicts, and frustrations and lovelessness. Until you purge yourself, you will remain his prisoner of negative love.

After a discussion based on these questions and with a mind revelation to aid in their recall, Chris, Nancy, and Laura were ready to write the Negative Emotional Autobiography with Father and then to experience father's bitch sessions. As with mother, only excerpts from their notes are given here.

By the time he finished his mother work, Chris had progressed enough to enable him to express his feelings more openly. After recalling 135 negative traits of his father, a well-known Protestant minister, he went back into his childhood and found the scenes in which his father exhibited them. Not surprisingly, Chris found that his father's negative traits (such as authoritarian, manipulative, uncaring, nonsupportive, critical, judgmental, invalidator, and many others) were a crucial influence in his emotional development during childhood. The few instances in which Chris rebelled against his father were either insignificant or unsuccessful, leading only to painful conflict.

When one adopts the same negative trait or admonition from both parents he suffers a compound emotional fracture. Chris's becoming a Zombie is a direct result of this trauma.

CHRIS, THE ZOMBIE
CONDENSED NEGATIVE EMOTIONAL
AUTOBIOGRAPHY WITH FATHER

When I was born, my father was in the process of fulfilling his idea of the way his life should be, which set the stage for the rest of my life with him. He hoped to manipulate, mold, and shape me to what he wanted and expected of me. When he couldn't, he showed disappointment and withdrew from me. He knew duty but love was only on "giving-to-get" terms. When he didn't get, he went off to his world audience and to his "good works."

Father was a large man, active and full of self-importance. He used to encourage me to play but only on his terms. I remember at age three at the beach I was to run to the water with him. I was afraid, so he made fun of me. My feelings weren't real; his were. His message was "Keep quiet and conform" by denying and invalidating myself.

The major theme running all through my life with my father was his nonsupport of me, my feelings, my needs. By direct or subtle means, his manipulation and authoritarianism structured my life. His indifference and neglect left me lonely and longing.

Dad was often the center of attention at gatherings, a fine singer, a good story-teller, and knowledgeable in discussions of world and religious affairs. Somehow I was always excluded. The son of a bitch gave lots of attention to everybody in his congregation but me.

He always seemed busy. After work he'd say hello, give a dutiful hug and kiss to my mother but usually not to me. I felt left out. I wanted a hug and kiss, too. I wanted to talk to him. He'd sit and read his newspaper until dinner, where conversation was limited to his ministry or the family, or about teaching me geography or vocabulary, or there were arguments over trivia. After dinner, either he went upstairs, closed his door, and worked on sermons (to instruct the world on how to love and have better marriages and raise children), or I was shuffled upstairs so he could give attention to a parishioner and I wasn't even permitted to come down to the kitchen for a glass of milk.

I learned how to hide my feelings early, certainly before age five. I decided: Don't trust him with my real perceptions or feelings, or he will invalidate them. He might rob me of those most precious experiences. He claimed to know better than I did what I felt, thought, and needed.

Dad was especially good working with people, for which he got lots of acclaim. I rebelled at his hypocrisy and began to dislike people. I withdrew into myself and became interested in mechanical things and science, where I could work alone. Dad had no interest in these pursuits. He was disappointed because I wasn't a leader in the neighborhood. I didn't play football or baseball well enough to lead the older and bigger boys, but father never took the time to teach me how to play better.

I often got his message: Be manly. Don't show hurt, fear, or be overemotional. When I was eight, I fell off the garage roof while showing off to get his attention. He carried me back to the house to help me get my wind back but showed no sympathy or warmth. Or when I cut my knee four inches to the bone, he carried me to the car and kept saying, "Be a big boy. Don't cry." I was glad he came to get me, but he blamed me for hurting myself and made me swallow my tears. He always inhibited my honest emotions, and I have had trouble in this area ever since.

My memory of one of my strongest, deepest moments of desperation and sorrow was probably duplicated many times. I am standing outside the door of Dad's bedroom where he is preparing a speech. I very much want and need his attention and love and have asked him something. I want him to share my excitement about a school accomplishment. Impatiently he says, "Stop, you're disturbing me. I have a lecture to work on. Now don't bother me again." I feel crushed. My head says, "He had work to do." My guts shout, "I'm worthless, he doesn't love me, never takes time. I only wanted a little bit of his time." But he wouldn't take two minutes for his only son.

He was manipulative and dishonest in his approach to me. He didn't respect me enough to be straight, though often I saw through it and was hurt and felt contempt for him. He gave me a sex book but did not share his feelings about sex, manhood, warmth, or father-son contact.

My parents never openly disagreed or argued. She gave in on almost everything. He "knew" it wasn't good for a child to hear his parents arguing. Just as I was excluded from his warmth and love, so I was excluded from seeing people honestly disagree and still get along. I still experience disagreement as dangerous and threatening, thanks to my unfatherly father.

My strongest experience with my father was when I was about eleven. He had been trying to get me to gain weight. (I wasn't OK as I was.) He decided I wasn't gaining because I was bad, deficient, lazy, unmotivated. I must gain one-half pound a day. Every morning for what seemed like months I was weighed and given a bare-assed swat for each one-half pound below his chart. I tried to gain, but I got sick. I would get up at five in the morning and drink quantities of water, fight not to vomit it all up, and go back to bed to appear asleep when he woke up. He felt guilty, so he told me he wanted to lose weight (true) and set a goal losing one pound a day. For each pound he was over, I was to swat him bare-assed with a bed slat. I knew he was doing that to ease his own conscience. I didn't want to hit my father—I still wanted to respect him—but when he insisted I hit him, I wanted to bash his Goddamned head to a bloody pulp. When he wouldn't let me out of the room until I did spank him, I finally would bash his ass as hard as I could, but it really didn't feel good. I wanted to shout how I hated his fucking guts right then, but I knew I was too scared.

The crowning blow, his abandonment of me and ultimate cop-out, was that he killed himself before my puberty by continuing to be overweight, ignoring his physician's statement that his heart was in critical condition. He worked long hours every day and had a heart attack in his pulpit, ironically preaching about how to live happy lives, conduct happy marriages, and love one another. He didn't even have the decency to die at home.

Chris's father taught him he must not show honest emotions. The feedback to Chris's father's work is similar in design and intent to the feedback on mother. Paragraph by paragraph Chris was made to see his father's overwhelming injustice and unloving treatment of him as a child. Chris was trained to be dead to emotional reality. He withdrew and became a Zombie. The feedback served to help jolt him out of his lassitude and unresponsiveness into anger at his bastard father. Years of pent-up tears and suppressed emotion were released.

A sampling of my remarks were: "You want to be loved, and your bastard father denied you your inalienable right to be loved by your parents. He really was a bastard father because it is obvious that you were literally unimportant to him."

"He ignored your existence," I told him angrily on tape. "You were only his puppet. Hell, Chris, you needed a loving father to depend on and look up to, not a puppeteer."

"The spanking episode showed he was a sado-masochist. Are you one now? That bastard's treatment of you was selfish and cruel. While presenting himself to the world as the benevolent, magnanimous church leader, in contrast he ran his home like an intellectual tyrant. Did he 'rule' with the firm hand of loving discipline? Certainly not. There was no loving manliness in his domination of his household. In truth he was a terribly unloving man who didn't trust others unless he was sure he could control their every move. It's difficult to believe that he was respected as an authority on love and marriage. He was really a case of the blind leading the blind. He was a nothing, zero father."

These words sound harsh and painful and they were intended to be. There had to be no doubt in Chris's mind how his bastard father failed. Like the cobbler's son who goes barefoot, Chris was the minister's son starved for love. His father bought the world's approval for his words of loving wisdom yet failed to practice what he preached. Again and again I reminded Chris that in the name of God's love his father had denied him a father's love. He never gathered the boy in his arms, kissed him and told him everything was all right, that Dad was there to love him and take care of him. Instead, Chris was brought up by a cold, authoritarian, hypocritical bastard.

The feedback triggered the redhot anger poor Zombie Chris had pent up for more than thirty years. Primed as he was by his painful memories, Chris had little trouble moving immediately to the bitch session. Afterward, he wrote his reaction to the first bitch session and transcribed the tape of a second bitch session on his own.

"Monday night, after the bitch session, I felt some releaf, I mean relief (good slip, 'leaf' as in healthy tree growth), also relieved at having expressed the inexpressible, vomited the unvomitable. Then, having generally recovered from the intensified sickness of the bitch session plus some riddance of the daddy-tied feeling—today, Wheeeeee!"

Here is a portion of his transcribed bitch session:

You bastard! I've been scared of you. I've been scared of people, scared of you—but no more! I'm not scared of you now. What do you think of that, you bastard?

You made me scared, *you authoritarian fucker. Telling me, "Leave me alone" or "Go see Mother." My mother could have been a woman. She could have loved . . . if you had cared . . . and had any balls . . . all you needed to do was love her and love me, listen to us, show us you cared. You'd come home . . . home! . . . That's supposed to be where there's* caring. *You'd come home, pick up your Goddamn paper, talk to mother, say to me, "Hello, how was your day?" and you'd walk out while I was telling you. You were supposed to listen, weren't you?*

You went out to get loved by the world because you couldn't take it from me. The only way I could get your attention was to screw up. You went off and you'd leave me. I hate your Goddamn gusts. I'd like to kill you!

All I wanted from you was warmth. I wanted you to see me. (Crying) I wanted you just to sit down and see what it was I was doing; give me credit. But no, you shit! You didn't have the time. You and your crusade to save the world for love, you phony fucker! (Crying)

Afraid of how other people would judge you, eh? You didn't care how I judged you. Well I judge you now: a nothing No Thing . . . No Person. No father. Nothing. *Self-centered, exhibitionistic zero! Big man! I was ten years old, and you put me down for not beating you up. Maybe that's what you wanted? That* is *what you wanted, Goddamn it! Well, it's what I want to do now. Then I didn't want to beat you. You intimidated me, and you shamed me, and you scared me, and you made me beat you on the butt with that Goddamned board, and the only thing I wanted was love. I didn't want to hit you . . . (Crying) . . . I wanted you to care.*

I hate you so fucking much! Well now I've got me a way to get it out. I'm going to throw up. I'm going to throw you up, as I couldn't do all those years. "Don't cry, be a man." Do you remember that? You didn't tell me not to throw up. No, you'd just spank me if I lost weight. And if I threw up all that water I was drinking, I'd lose weight. You taught me . . . you taught me to keeeeeeeep down all that shit. No more. You can be what you are for the next hundred years . . . stink in it . . . no more for me . . . no more . . . I've had enough.

Intellectualizing son of a bitch! I'm going to get you out of me for good . . . and I will not let you back in. No, no, not ever again . . . no more. I won't let you in again, you shit!

After I finished, I went to my sanctuary and my child looked down at my "father" who is still tied, curled up and protecting his head, bruised, quiet. On my instruction, my guide drags him/it bodily out. I thought about helping drag it, but realized I really didn't want to get that close to the S.O.B. now. He's left still tied on the ground outside as my guide and I shut the door together. I find I am breathing deeply of the air in my sanctuary and this time feeling fantastically relieved. My legs are still shaking, and I feel weak, but God do I feel more solid, more my own man, stiff and sore muscles, but lighter and freer somehow.

Ironically, when you get the hate out in the open like this and clear it, you can accomplish more than dutifully following the Biblical admonition to honor your father. You can indeed *learn* to *love* him honestly, as subsequent chapters will confirm.

NANCY, THE HOSTILE

Nancy saw less of her father during her childhood than Chris saw of his, but she was nonetheless emotionally devastated by the negative impact he had on her. Her father deserted the family when she was three, and yet she found seventy-one negative traits, moods, and admonitions she attributed to him. She adopted forty-six of father's negative traits and rebelled against the other twenty-five. Until she wrote her Negative Emotional Autobiography with Father and heard my feedback, she believed her father had been only a minor influence in her life, since he wasn't much a part of her life. In truth, her father played a most important role in her negative development, particularly in the development of her traits of anger and hostility towards men. Her father's angry moods were more overt than those of her mother and dominated the household atmosphere. Her father was also the source of the message that her mother and all women, including Nancy herself, were worthless and that it was a woman's lot in life to be abandoned by men. She rejected herself because of her father's rejection of her and subsequently married two men who shared her father's negative attitude toward women. Inevitably the marriages *ended* in rejection. In these excerpts from her Negative Emotional Autobiography with Father, Nancy realizes how traumatic their brief time together had been and how, through the negative love pattern, her father continued to be the dominant force in her adult life. After returning psychically to the time before her birth, she wrote:

> *My father was surprised when my mother told him she was pregnant. He had been ignoring her, involved in his business, going to whore-houses because he'd lost interest in her. So he was dismayed and worried about the likely expenses. She'd had a terrible time giving birth to my brothers, and he considered my existence an inescapable evil in a life full of irritations.*
>
> *When I was first born, he paid no attention to me at all except for a feeling of relief that it had been an easy birth after all, and my mother could now get back to her duties without too much difficulty, and his life wouldn't be disrupted too much. I yearned for my daddy, but he quite literally never touched me or spoke to me until I was past a year old. I would feel his presence sometimes, nodding approvingly, making phony affectionate sounds since I was never presented to him unless I was dressed up nicely. He talked about me, though, and admired me as the "baby," and immediately*

insisted that my three-year-old brother have his hair cut short and start acting and be disciplined like a boy since he was no longer the baby in the family. That resulted in my brother Walter's resenting me violently all his life.

When I started to be responsive and began walking, he began occasionally to pet me and play with me as one would with a puppy or kitten. When he was in the mood, I would be swung up on his broad shoulders and feel his warmth. I would be his darling and his baby, and he became so terribly important to me! He was full of strength and vitality. But it was a seesaw love. Available sometimes, for reasons I didn't understand, then not there. I'd imagine that I had done something wrong to lose him, that there was something wrong with me.

There were few open quarrels between him and my mother in those days. Mostly I remember his bad temper, his constant demands, his disinterest in her as a person, and her hurt silences and tears in the night. I knew Daddy didn't love her and I was unsure of his love for me.

As a businessman he was downright stupid, mostly brought on by his bullheaded conviction that he was always right and his decisions had to be correct. He had difficulty supporting us, changing jobs often. He had so much anger in him that he was often battling with those he worked with. We had to move three times before I was three—always to worse places—following his different jobs. There was never a feeling of security in the home. He was moody, irritable, subject to unexplained changes that would throw the whole family into a new environment. I was scared of him so often.

But he was sometimes loving to me, and as I grew a little older, I was delightedly conscious of my special place as his pet, and I adored and feared him at the same time. On the Christmas just before I was three he made a wooden slide in the basement for my brother and me. I was proudly given the first ride, lifted to the top by him. I ran a large splinter into my behind. He had wanted to give us

something impressive, but he hadn't even been care-
ful enough to see that we wouldn't be hurt on it.
He laid me over his knee and took it out, and I was
aware of my mother's anger at him and my own
pain and his being the source of it, and feeling
confused and torn up inside and still wanting to be
close to him.

Then we packed up for a long trip to Wisconsin.
Just the three kids and my mother went. We were
to enter my brothers in school, and he was going
to join us as soon as his present business venture
permitted because he was going to work in Wiscon-
sin. He kissed me and hugged me and said he'd be
coming real soon, and I believed him.

He never came. One thing after another held
him up, and the years went by. He never even
came to visit. He didn't send enough money to
support us, and my mother had to go to work. He
abandoned us. He didn't want us. The stupid, in-
sensitive, uncaring bastard!! He was so involved in
himself, so convinced of his own importance that
he could rationalize his treatment of us. And he
knew that my mother was a child emotionally and
couldn't take care of us. He just didn't care. He
knew she couldn't earn more than starvation wages.
He knew how unhappy she was and that we had to
live with that. All the warmth and love he gave me
had been a lie. He didn't really care at all.

When I was five and a half, my mother deter-
mined to go back and force him to take on his
family again. When we got to the house where he
was living, my mother sent me ahead to announce
our arrival. After recovering from the shock, he did
pick me up to hug me. I felt a clutching in my
throat, so I turned my head away as I'd been
taught, not to cough in his face. He didn't under-
stand, and we had a brief tussle, him pulling me
toward him, my pulling away. Then he sat me down
in dismissal, and I never again got to be hugged or
kissed. I know now I couldn't handle my yearning
for him and rage at his having left us.

So we all moved in together, and unpleasant

*scenes between him and my mother punctuated
our days. We all knew that he liked some other
woman better than my mother. I could hear it in
his voice, and sense it in his actions. And I was no
longer his pet; his response to me was merely perfunctory. At first I yearned so for him to pay attention to me, but he simply acted as if I were one
more female too many. He gave my brothers each
a puppy, and I was supposed to be content with
the kitten my aunt brought me six weeks later. He
took my brothers on an outing to the Statue of
Liberty, and I had to spend the day in my aunt's
lamp shop. I learned from him then what a disaster
it is to be female, how much I missed out on because I wasn't one of his sons.*

*Once my mother told my brothers to do the
dishes, and my father announced grandly that he
was going to be a millionaire—and the sons of a
millionaire did not have to do dishes. What about
the wife of a millionaire? What about the daughter
of a millionaire?*

*Once I was under the kitchen table when my
father came into the room. I stayed there, hidden,
shaking with fear and hating him as he yelled at
my mother, pounding on the table with his fist.*

*A little while after that my mother and brothers
and I moved again. I don't even remember saying
good-bye to him. I was scared of the unknown we
were going into but glad to be leaving him. I hated
him. I didn't want to be around him anymore.*

*From that time on we were alone. The com-
munication, if any, between him and my mother
was a mystery to me. I received no word from him,
not so much as a card on my birthday or on
Christmas.*

*Five years later, back in New York, my mother
tried to force him to help support us. There was
some kind of court scene. I remember sitting outside with my brother, and I saw him go in. I made
no effort to speak to him and turned my head
away. I never saw him again after that. He died
when I was seventeen, and I didn't attend his*

funeral because we were in California by then. I didn't want to, anyhow.

In response to Nancy's father's work I validated her perception and supported her new understanding that her father's uncaring behavior had devastating results for everyone in the family. His rejection and abandonment left physical marks of loneliness and unhappiness on her beautiful but unresponsive face.

Although she hardly needed much reminding, I stressed again and again what a rotten, no-good bastard her father had been to her and the rest of the family; how his angry behavior planted the seeds of her insecurity and lack of self-assurance particularly around men. At my urging she went more deeply into recalling scenes in which her father angrily pounded the table and yelled, which served to focus her rage against his loud, violent assaults on the family. I used the incident with the splinter in her buttocks to demonstrate her evident masochism in relating to men. After some honest introspection she acknowledged that being hurt by men was relating in negative love to her father.

"He was a penny-ante Hitler," I said. "A big Daddy-O, a real zero who forced his wife and children to obediently walk on eggshells. He put you on a seesaw of love, giving you occasional love and then dropping you on your emotional ass. Because of that bastard you never knew which end was up, and you still don't!"

I called her on her mistaken belief that it would have been better to have been a son to this bastard father of hers and called attention to her masculine mode of dress and mannerisms. I reminded her that her brothers had been in terrible emotional shape all their lives because of his treatment of them, that her misfortune was not that she was born a female but that she was fathered by a scoundrel and a bully. In every possible way I encouraged her to see her father as he really was in all his negativity. Her anger and resentment steadily rose to fever pitch and burst forth like a fiery volcano on bitch night. Out of every negative comes a positive. Her adopted covert hostility became overt and in the bitch session she was freed of the negating aspect of hostility.

At the end of her bitch session, Nancy wrote, "I'm going down in the basement now and get a brick, and mark your face in the dirt, and pound on it until I feel clean. I went down and made a face in the dirt—your face, with eyes and mouth, and pounded on it with a brick until it was just a bloody pulp. I drew your face again and smashed it once for my mother who mourned you all of her life. After I was finished, I came upstairs and vomited and felt that I was vomiting you from out of every cell of my body."

At my suggestion Nancy did a mind revelation in which her guide brought father into her sanctuary.

> *I am in my sanctuary. My guide sends out my adult intellectual self, leaving the negative child at age thirteen. He produces father, immobilized. My first reaction is to spit in his face. Then I think of Bob's suggestion to vomit on him, and I do. It comes from my toes, streams and streams of vile-looking yellowish and greenish gunk. It goes on and on, finally leaving me empty and white and shaken. My guide removes my father and helps me out of my soiled clothes. First I wash off in the nearby ocean, and then we go to my healing pool. I feel tears in my eyes as my guide walks with his arm supportively around my shoulders. He bathes me in the healing pool, washing my hair and letting water run from his cupped palm over my face in a half-playful fashion. Afterward he gives me a costume of soft, clean blue, like the one he gave me at our first meeting. I rest in the sun. My adult self quietly joins me. I feel calm and free. Father can no longer control me with invisible negative love strings.*

LAURA, THE BAYGULL

Like Nancy and all other little girls, Laura's first male love in her life had been her father. Yet her emotional life as a woman was blighted, because her father never returned the love she instinctively felt for him. She was painfully aware of his rejection of her. The truth of her negative love for him made shocking sense—after she compiled his list of more than

400 negative traits, she realized she had adopted 325 of them into her personality. She was her father all over again. Ugh!

> *I am three years old. I visualize myself standing in the living room, watching my daddy read the paper. He has no time for me. I am two years old, sleeping on the couch while my father reads his paper. I am one year old, sitting in the grass with my mother while my daddy takes my picture. I am two months old. My daddy is taking my picture. I am about to be born. I am eight, seven, six, five, four, three months old. How do I feel?*
>
> *I am a three-month fetus. I hear my father shouting. He is saying, "Goddamnit, Alice, I don't want any children. You talk to Mrs. Jones and find out who did her abortion. I want you to get an abortion." I am shocked. Why does my father want to kill me? What have I done to him that he hates me so much? My mother is crying. She defies him, and the rift in the family begins.*
>
> *I am six months old. I just kicked my mother, and she is excited. She wants my daddy to put his hand on her stomach and feel me move. Daddy says, "That's silly. All babies move. So what?" I wish my daddy would put his hand on me. I would like him to touch me.*
>
> *I am born, and my father is upset that I am a girl. He had his heart set on a boy. At least then he would have a pal, as he has never had any friends. He believes that my mother and I have played a nasty trick on him because I am female. If I had only been a boy, then maybe he could have loved me. I feel rejected. Being female is not OK. I begin to cry.*
>
> *I am a year old. My mother leaves me with the neighbor couple while she goes shopping. The man plays with me. He puts a nickel on my toe, and it falls off. I laugh and laugh. I wish my daddy would play with me like that. Why doesn't he ever take care of me? I wish my daddy would take care of me.*
>
> *I am three years old. My daddy gives me a nickel*

every Saturday for washing his back. He puts the nickel on top of the refrigerator so that I have to climb on a big chair to reach it. I wish my daddy would give me a big hug instead of money.

We are out for a Sunday drive. I am riding in the back, as usual. I want to sit in the front seat between my folks, like a love sandwich, Daddy—me— Mommy. My daddy always insists that I ride in back because I wiggle too much.

I am in the garage, watching my daddy work. He has such lovely tools. He has a cabinet full of hammers, screwdrivers, files, cans of nails, big boxes with interesting things like a lathe for mending shoes, and an emery wheel. My daddy is always busy and doesn't notice me. I begin to dump out the screws. He tells me I'm in the way, to run along and play. I would like to work with my daddy, to learn all about the different tools. But he is always too busy, too irritable. He makes me a lovely wooden teeter-totter. It is always leaning up against the wall in the garage. I want to play with it, but daddy says it is too much trouble to get out the saw horse and it might slip. Finally, I learn not to ask to play with the lovely teeter-totter. I am a good girl and don't want to rock the boat.

I am five years old and starting to school. My daddy decides I should get a whole dime for my allowance instead of a nickel. But I must do something to earn it. He wants me to be his detective and tell on mother if she does something she doesn't want him to know about. One Saturday we are at the dinner table. My daddy wants to know whether I'm going to do my "detectin'." I whisper in his ear that mother and I went to the movies out of the grocery money this week. Both of my parents get angry, and I am in the middle. I feel that my daddy has tricked me into being a tattle-tale. My mother spanks me for telling a secret. If my daddy were not so stingy, we would not have to sneak around. If my mother were not afraid of him, we would not have to try to fool my daddy. We are all unhappy. My father has used me as a dupe. He does not respect me.

I am six and in the first grade. I am in a little play at school, but my daddy doesn't come. Later, I am in an evening program (or was supposed to be except that I have a big bandage on my eye where I got hit in the head with a baseball bat). My whole class is doing a Maypole dance, except me. My mother has made almost all the costumes. My mother and the neighbor girl and I go. My father is not there. I participate in many activities at school. My father is never at PTA, does not help with Bluebirds or Campfire Girls like my mother does. At church the Baptist preacher asks me to recite the Christmas story, which I know by heart. I do this in front of the whole congregation. My father is not there.

I am nine. We are getting ready to go to a movie. My mother and I are waiting in the car for my father to come out. He has to go to the garage, get a clean handkerchief, go to the bathroom, get a cookie, etc., etc. At last he is in the car. We will be late for the beginning of the picture. My mother is mad. My father is eating an apple and ignoring her. They have already had a disagreement about what movie to see. My mother wants to see a comedy, and he has given in. The movie is very funny. My daddy slaps his knee, stomps his feet, and snorts. We come out of the movie. My mother says, "How did you like it?" He says flatly, "It was OK." I wonder why he won't say he liked it. What is wrong with having fun?

I am twelve years old. My father is teasing me again. He gouges too deep and hurts me. I scratch him with my fingernails and blurt out, "I hate you." He is thunderstruck; so am I. I know that I shouldn't say this, shouldn't criticize my parent, should honor my father. I stick this thought back down inside. I never bring it up again.

When my menstrual cycle begins, my father makes no comment. He never talks about sex except to make some remark, such as, "New York is sin city. All the people are immoral there. I can't

understand why my sisters want to live there." He
reads an article on sex and then says, "That's the
filthiest thing I ever read." He is no help to me at
all in discovering my womanhood. He is tight-
lipped and rigid about sex. He equates pleasure
with sin. I feel there is something bad about me.
My father is ashamed of my femaleness.

In her feedback I encouraged Laura to feel the depths of
her yearning for her father, again to experience fully the
little baby in her crying out, "Daddy, Daddy, where are you?
I need you. Where are you?" Before summoning forth the
buried rage, it is often necessary to recognize and give voice
to the loneliness and deprivation suffered by the negative
emotional child. After such an experience longing and yearning turn to justifiable accusation and rage.

Even after she recognized her father's rejection of her,
Laura's response to it was always muted by the Baygull programming she received from her mother. With every line she
wrote I stressed his cold and inhuman treatment of her, his
stinginess, his heartless stomping on her expectations of love
from him. He put her on a seesaw of love by letting her wash
his back and then making the nickel reward difficult to reach.
Why did he build a teeter-totter and then not allow her to
use it? Because God forbid she should get hurt using it, then
he would feel doubly guilty for causing her injury *and* for
not wanting her to be born in the first place. I goaded her
with:

"Not only did he deprive you of his love, he tainted your
relationship with your mother by coaxing you to spy on her.
That bastard gave you no brothers or sisters, no real father,
and then he topped it off by trying to destroy your relationship with your mother. Too much!"

"Why couldn't he let you sit between you and Mommy in
the front seat? Did he hate you that much that he had to
stick you in the back seat? Didn't he know all you wanted
was attention? You're a procrastinator. You're never on time.
Where do you think you learned that negative trait? From
that bastard who was always late. 'See, Daddy, if I'm late
just like you, I won't outdo you, *now* will you love me?'
Remember the times you went to the movies, and how he
found excuses to delay? Today you are *always* late out of

negative love to Daddy."

"How do you suppose you learned your perfectionism? You feel that nothing you ever do is right. He would *permit* you to mow the lawn, but he made you do it two or three times. It had to be perfect or Daddy wouldn't love you. You have had to do everything over and over again to be perfect like your bastard Daddy demanded. Your present perfectionism is one of your heaviest energy drains, thanks to Daddy."

As the story of Laura's barren relationship with her father unfolded, her resentment of him became more open. With the bitch session, the time had come for her to allow the rage and hatred to spew forth. While most people find it easier to bitch at father than at mother, a few find that their fear of him is so inhibiting that they choke up. In cases like Laura's it takes great patience and effort by both the teacher and client to open to the repressed anger and permit the catharsis of the bitch session. During the bitch session at the Center she sat immobilized, insisting that she felt nothing. Rather than confront her resistance directly, I asked her to describe what she sensed was holding her back. Here's what she wrote:

> *What is holding me back from bitching? Two things that I can think of straight off, which are really aspects of the same thing. First, I am paralyzed with fear of men—my father to begin with, Jack my lover, and all men after that. This makes me afraid to bitch. It also makes me afraid to lose what I have—half a man, a crumb of a man, any shred of love I have or ever have had at all.*
>
> *The second thing holding me back is the deep depression I've been in all week, which is precisely my sickness. This is my feeling, a deep conviction reinforced by years of negative thinking, that I never have been and never will be loved by a man. This overwhelming sense of emptiness, this pure need which has never been satisfied.*
>
> *I have the feeling of being congenitally unlovable where men are concerned. All my life, since before my memory, I have felt inadequate, a zero, totally devoid of lovableness. I feel that it is totally impossible for me to have a loving relationship with*

a man I care about. Someone I don't care for might say he loved me, but it would be only words. In the areas where it counts, down where I live, I am convinced, I know that I can never be loved by a man I care about.

This black depression becomes a trap. Because of my intense, lifelong need for a man's love, I come on too strong, too needy, too helpless and hopeless. Men run in panic from this need which threatens to strangle and smother them. They can't or won't deal with it. Consequently, the greater the need, the greater the likelihood of my not getting it satisfied.

As Jack did not want to see me this week, his little "rejection" cast me into a funk—the "nobody loves me" syndrome. Of course he doesn't. Who wants a teary-eyed woman to make him feel guilty? Bitching at father makes it seem as if I am rejecting Jack, who is so much like father, and who is my last man, my last hope. Half a man but better than none! The thought of losing the little I have makes me feel stifled, drained of energy, unable to bitch or get through the Process. I feel as if I'm being smothered, can't breathe.

After this special exercise and a further mind revelation, Laura emotionally accepted the truth: all her current problems were rooted in her father's failure to love her. With our support she was able to vent her pain and rage. Her anguished wordless howls bore testimony to the pain she had suppressed for thirty-five years. Laura had many other bitch sessions that week, each directed at the specific scenes and traits she had previously recalled. Here is a small portion of one of those sessions:

Daddy, you dutiful, cold bastard, I hate you for all the times you gave me your duty. **Your fucking duty. Shove your fucking duty.** *How cold, narrow, sterile and unprofitable is your Goddamn duty. May you roast in hell for all the dutiful things you did for me—for your dutiful house, and dutiful meals, and dutiful clothes, etc., etc.* **Crap on your** dutiful shit! *If you'd ever given me* **one ounce** *of love or caring or support, if you'd ever given me a shred of warm, tender, caring recognition with all your duty, it might have passed as at least pseudo-love and I could have grown up secure. You son of a bitch. You stood in my way. You planted your feet and deliberately blocked my way. You with your sour face and sour looks and sour personality. The only word in your vocabulary was "no." You could never smile and say "yes." It can't be done says you. Bullshit!* It **can** *be done. It* will *be done. I shall live, am living, have lived in spite of you. If you don't like it you can shove it up your ass!*

The biggest thing I hate about you is the feeling you gave me of being abandoned, rejected, a zero, a nothing. I won't have it. I won't have it anymore! Instead of thinking of myself as nothing, as unworthy of love, of concern, of caring, I'll think of myself as a loving, caring, cared-for person that other people like. How do you like that? You don't like it do you? You wanted me to go through life miserable, lonely, without a friend. Well, tough shit! It's too late because I've declared my autonomy from you. I won't be you anymore—self-rejecting, cold, unapproachable, snobbish, too good to speak to anyone. I won't be a masochist for you. I won't think of myself as miserable, a failure, a person that no one could ever love. Just because you didn't love me, you bastard, doesn't mean someone else won't. And I'm going to love him back, too—more than I ever loved you.

I want to be free of you. I am *free of you. Get your rigor mortis fingers off of me. I'm giving your corpse a proper burial. I am slamming down the lid of the coffin myself. "Let the dead bury the dead." Like Ruth coming out of the land of Moab, leaving the dead behind, I shall enter into a new land where love is waiting. So be it. Go to hell, Daddy!*

To integrate further the effects of her bitching at father, I asked Laura to do a mind revelation in which she asked her child to tell her intellect how she felt after bitching at father. This is what she wrote:

> *I feel that father is no longer a threat to me. I see him there with his hands and feet tied to the stake (in her sanctuary), but he seems limp, unreal, like a ghost that turns out to be a sheet flapping in the wind, a corpse who is gone and has left behind only his shroud. There is nothing there. He is gone, who knows where? He was a towering monster, a King Kong, a hairy beast terrifying me with his roar. Then he became a tiny pip-squeak, a midget, a belch, a fart, a stink. Then he shrank away even farther to nothing. He doesn't terrify me anymore. I was paralyzed with fear, rabid with rage, indignant, victimized, frustrated. Now I can scarcely care. He is a rag flapping in the wind, a scarecrow. Who's afraid of a scarecrow? Who's afraid of the big, bad wolf? He's a fairy tale. A tale told by an idiot. Insane sanity. Illogical logic. I'm no longer afraid of his power. He's an imaginary bully. I said, "Boo!" to him—and he vanished.*

Bitching done, Laura joined Chris and Nancy in a space similar to the one experienced after having bitched at mother. They were totally relieved of the burden of their parental repressed childhood anger—but they were not yet finished with father.

CHAPTER IX

"TELL ME I MAY
SPONGE AWAY THE WRITING
ON THIS STONE!"

"I don't believe it is possible to defend that bastard," is a usual and often-voiced refrain. Father's Defense, like that of mother, requires an abrupt shift of view. All their lives Baygulls and Zombies have been denied the expression of their latent anger and resentment harbored toward father. They are so elated after being freed of the years of oppression and inhibition that they are reluctant to move on.

To be effective the change must be abrupt. Turning the coin to see its other side is a 180-degree shift. The bitching at father is only one-sided. The sudden shift to the other side drives home the impact of this defense in a way that a gradual shift of view would not. It is necessary to be catapulted into the bitching at father and then catapulted into defending him in order to shatter negative complacency. Bitching at father brings power and autonomy, while defending him transcends denunciation and replaces it with understanding and compassion. For he too has a diamond-essence spiritual self, albeit covered heavily by his negative patterns.

Yes, father, like mother, is guilty for not consistently loving you and he, too, is *blameless*. To feel this and stop blaming him is a crucial step in being free of his contribution to your negative love programming. One of the great ironies of the negative love syndrome is that children learn to blame and carry grudges from—who else?—mother and father. If those two never forgave an insult or overlooked a misdeed, how could their children do otherwise than show the same lack of compassion and tolerance? If the parents never gave of themselves in a positive way, how could the children give positively to the parents in return? What tragic injustice for everyone!

Those who carry grudges and nurse resentments often do so out of obedience to a parental admonition, either silent or overt, such as, "Don't let anyone get away with anything." Hostiles often have difficulty defending father for this reason. They need to be reminded that nursing self-righteous anger is derived from a negative trait of either mother or father.

Baygulls usually have a different problem. Mother and father's admonishments have been something like, "You should forgive people when they sin or do wrong. Be bigger than they are by forgiving them." Living by this directive serves the dual purpose of allowing the Baygull to feel superior while garnering the undeserved admiration of those who are fooled by his or her apparent phony piety. While appearing more pleasant than the Hostile, the Baygull's generous pose is just another false ego trip.

If you are a Zombie, however, you were probably programmed by your parents with such commands as, "Be quiet. Be safe. Don't show your feelings, no matter what." So the Zombie may have difficulty first bitching at father and then later defending him. Fortunately, once the *feeling* level is contacted (it's always there), the energy behind it, like that of a flowing river current, can be rechanneled into another course and the Zombie can experience father's positive defense.

As with mother, a series of powerful mind revelations creates the Defense of Father. Seeing and hearing father as an adolescent boy describing his relationship with his mother and father is a totally moving, enlightening experience. The conversation with the thirteen-year-old child of father expands the view of him to encompass his total being. Children usually see their fathers only in the roles they portrayed rather than as complete people. Yet a person is not the roles he plays. By definition, the roles are what he is *not* and must learn to unlearn. If father actually were a loving man, for example, he would not have to play a role. He would simply *be* a loving man.

While your father had many adult roles to play (father

husband, son, boss or employee, taxpayer, tourist, buyer, seller, doctor, lawyer, teacher, engineer, student, or whatever), that was only a small part of who he really was. For all his bluff and bluster, or meek silence, your father also had an unloved, frustrated child inside him. It is the same child who in each of us longs only to love and be loved. And within the big man who made your life hell was a frightened, angry, lost, lonely little boy who lived through a hell of his own and never recovered from it. The adult father you knew was also an extension of a frightened, unloved, unfulfilled youngster just like you once were. For in truth your father was a victim of negative love patterns as you were and perhaps even more so. He acted no more from his adult free will in treating you unlovingly than you act from your adult free will in not loving those around you. And he had no choice but to pass his negative patterns on to you.

Father did not love you consistently and positively because no one ever loved him consistently and positively. He therefore could not love you. It was beyond his limited ability as an emotional being to give you the warmth and emotional goodness you needed from a father. To continue to blame him is to show him an even greater injustice than he showed you. Love comes out of the fullness of one's being, never from the emptiness.

Father's Defense does not saddle you with the Christian admonition, "turn the other cheek," but creates an emotional, intellectual, and spiritual experience of father's love tragedy so that you can *feel* compassion for him at *all* levels. Experiencing father's suffering, rather than merely intellectualizing it, brings resentment and anger to an end and paves the way to self-acceptance and self-love.

The Defense of Father is the same as the Defense of Mother in its three parts. First the negative emotional child psychically confronts the thirteen-year-old child of his father in the sanctuary. "Child of my father," he asks, "what was your childhood like? Where and how did you learn the negative traits I adopted from you?" The mind or psyche of his father then relates the specifics that created his childhood programming and who made him the man he was. They converse in dialogue fashion, with father's child answering the specific questions put to him about the origin of each of his negative traits. The client's child relentlessly pursues understanding by asking questions like, "Where did you learn to be undemonstrative?", etc.

With the information uncovered in the dialogue, father's Trinity then dictates the story of his negative emotional autobiography in more orderly fashion; the result is more moving emotional understanding. This monologue is then followed by the Trial-log, the second "day in court" for the negative emotional child to bitch at father. In this procedure father, with his new understanding of his childhood programming, is able to defend himself. Should the client's negative emotional child get out of line, the spiritual self is present to act as judge-moderator to oversee the Trial-log. After these three experiences one emotionally arrives at a positive place of understanding with no condemnation and compassion for father.

At this point in their Process work, Chris, Laura, and Nancy have finished bitching at father and are feeling the exaltation of their apparent victory over his lifelong negative influence.

Communicating with his father's thirteen-year-old child self, Chris's child learned that his father's early programming at home had been even more Zombie-like than his mother's. Chris's paternal grandfather had been a businessman, involved in running community affairs and aloof and withdrawn from his family. His creed had been work, duty, and propriety. At home he was emotionally absent, choosing to retreat from his son and daughters behind a wall of papers and books. While he was the image of manliness to the world, at home he was subservient to his wife, who ruled the house.

Chris's paternal grandmother, the source of the other half of his father's negative love programming, dominated his father's upbringing. "A self-righteous prig" was the way Chris's father described her in their dialogue. "She spent all her time on community projects and charities, so I had to fend for myself. She didn't believe in 'coddling or caressing children,' so I learned early that crying would not get me warmth." Later, his mother taught him to be condescending toward others and to behave in a cold, smooth, studied way that would bring "credit" to her. She used to paralyze him with her critical stares. To gain what few crumbs of approval she offered, he learned to achieve and be a leader, do his duty and ignore his own feelings and needs. Chris learned that his father was the son of an authoritarian woman who demanded that he deny his own feelings and live according to hers.

Experiencing the kind of parents his father had, Chris was able to make sense of the web of negative love passed on from generation to generation. His father, like him, was programmed by both his mother and father to be a Zombie, feeling little and emotionally expressing even less. By understanding why his father programmed him as he did, Chris was able to substitute compassion for his dead father in place of the life-long anger.

Integrating what he learned in his father's defense with what he already knew about his mother, Chris was further able to see how both his parents had been programmed to be superior, unfeeling, undemonstrative, overly concerned with appearances, and unloving. While there were some differences in the programming of his mother and father, in many crucial ways each reinforced the "Zombieism" of the other. The negative traits which plagued Chris, his lack of trust, impatience, snobbishness, and overall critically disapproving, unemotional pose, were now traced back two generations on both sides of his family. In seeing the full negative love pattern spread out before him, and enduring the catharsis of first rage and then compassionate understanding for his mother and father, Chris removed the roots of his negative programming and prepared to move to the next stage of learning how to love.

Nancy also achieved a profound understanding of her negative patterns through her dialogue with young Charles, her father's child at puberty. She listened as he dictated the story of his hard life as a poor farm boy in Kansas and, later, of the rigors and deprivations of life in the working-class slums of Pittsburgh.

"My father was a hard, tough man," the child of father told Nancy's child, "a heavy drinker who disciplined us with his fists when we didn't jump to obey him. He was an angry man, and it seemed to me that he took little pleasure in his family or in anything in life except getting drunk, spinning off at the mouth and playing cards. Sometimes I thought that he didn't know our names."

He explained that he had been the sixth of nine children, just one of the middle children in a large family that treated children as economic burdens and, later, as economically exploitable resources.

Young Charles also told Nancy how his mother had been a strong, willful woman who silently resented his father for not giving her the luxuries she wanted. It was she who had engineered their move to Pittsburgh, and the children knew her as the real power in the house. Charles had briefly felt his mother's tenderness toward him during his infancy, only to be rudely supplanted by the next child as he was passed on to the uncertain care of the older children.

He also related to Nancy the misery of their unstable, precarious life as a working-class family in Pittsburgh. Two of the younger children had died before age five, and Charles felt his parents would not have cared if he had died, either. Loud, angry quarrels between his mother and father were an almost daily event in his home. His mother would castigate his father in front of the children, while manipulating the children into giving her the approval she failed to get from her husband.

Once she heard her father's story of deprivation and anguish, Nancy was able to see and feel the total truth—Charles passed on to her the hurts from negative love inflicted on him as a boy. Nancy's father's physical desertion of her mother, for example, had duplicated her grandfather's psychological desertion of her grandmother. Out of negative love to grandfather, her father had obeyed the silent but clear admonition, "Women and children are a burden. It's best to withdraw from them." Emotionally experiencing her father as a young boy weeping with tears of frustration and loneliness served to trigger Nancy's own tears of compassion and sadness for the tragedy of her late father. Sadly, she faced another truth. Father died an unloving and unloved child, boy and man.

When Laura came to her Trial-log, she, too, understood her father but had not completely lost her desire to condemn him for the hurts she suffered at his hand. In the Trial-log her child self had another opportunity to attack her father, only this time he was permitted to defend himself against her charges. With the occasional help of her spiritual self as judge-moderator, Laura eventually relinquished her anger at father and replaced it with honest understanding.

Among other things, she learned how and where her father had bitterly learned his pattern of rejection. When her father, George, had been an infant, her grandfather had deserted the family and fled to another state. News arrived soon afterward that he had shot himself to death. While growing up, Laura had heard the story of her grandfather's suicide, but hearing her father's thirteen-year-old self tell it as he experienced it emotionally gave it a new dimension. What George explained, which she had not known before, was that he blamed himself for his father's death; that he believed during his childhood that his birth was too much for his father to handle, which caused his father's desertion and self-destruction.

"I always felt that if I hadn't been born," he told Laura psychically, "he might have stayed with my mother and the other children. Maybe they would have had a better life if I hadn't come along to be another mouth to feed, another demand put on him. If only I hadn't driven my father away!" Talking to the guilt-ridden child her father had been, Laura felt with him the hopelessness and self-hatred he had lived with all his life. While recognizing the error in his belief that he was responsible for his father's desertion, she was also able to see that her father had lived his life as if this were *true.* For the first time she was able to enter into his experience and see the world as he did.

Little George described his mother as if she had been the old woman who lived in a shoe, with too many children and too much to do. He grew up feeling that life was a struggle and that laughter and pleasure were wrong and out of place. He learned from his mother (Laura's grandmother) to lose himself in his work and avoid painful feelings. George's mother programmed him to live by the old ethic of hard work and little display of emotions.

From her grandfather Laura's father learned to abandon his family. George's father had physically abandoned his family, while George psychologically abandoned his daughter. Laura grew up feeling torn by her father's lack of love and acceptance, while resentfully believing that he could have given it to her if he had wanted to. After her father's defense, however, she understood that his programming from her grandparents left him totally incapable of loving himself, his wife, his daughter, or anyone else. He had received so many negative messages from his parents that he could only pass rejection along to his children. In attempting to rebel against her father's negative behavior and self-hatred, Laura adopted her mother's Baygull false buoyancy and cheer. Thus, Laura learned through the negative love pattern from her parents to tightly restrain her feelings of anger and hatred behind a mask of good cheer and ready smiles. She could not win, but to lose.

As father's prosecution must be real to be cathartic so too must his defense be real to have permanent positive effect. After the moving experience of his defense one is able to feel for the poor negatively programmed emotional child still trapped within father the adult. The experience of feeling his tragedy must be so deep and intense that it makes an indelible imprint on the psyche, assuring that anger and resentment toward father are banished forever.

Father's compassion session creates the compelling emotional experience necessary to replace the anger with tender feelings. As with mother, the purpose is not just to feel grief over his death, but to evoke overwhelming grief and despair over the pathetic tragedy of father's living life without love and fulfillment. Experiencing father's wasted life, the client can take a giant step closer to loving him.

Like the others, Nancy experienced her father dying in the present, as a grown man with a little lonely boy trapped within him. She felt deep sadness, longing and futility—not for herself, but for the poor man lying in his casket, a man who lived unloved and unloving. The compassion aroused in Nancy, as in all others who do this Process, was very moving. Her father had actually died during her adolescence, yet she was able to reexperience him dying in the present and feel for him as if his death had just occurred. These moments of sadness and pain, *for* father rather than *because* of him, consolidated Nancy's new feeling space. The funeral scene with father also helped motivate Nancy to rededicate herself to avoiding father's tragedy in her own life. She committed herself to finding peace and love. Here is a portion of Nancy's experience of her father's funeral scene:

> *The attendants lower the coffin into the freshly dug grave and it comes to rest. I pick up a handful of dirt and let it fall through my fingers. As it hits the top of the coffin, I see the boy within the man, dead inside. My tears are streaming down my cheeks one after another faster than I can wipe them away.*

Poor hopeless little boy. You never stood a chance. Who mourns you? You had three children, yet except for me they neither know nor care that you are gone, and if they did, they would send a curse after you. Who has loved you, self-centered little boy having to pretend to be a man? You hated and mistreated us just as you were hated and mistreated by your parents. Now you are dead and this life's chance is gone. (Sobbing) You didn't want things to be this way! I wish I could help you! I want to help you. I want things to have been different for you. Oh, Daddy! Oh, Daddy! How I wish it could have all been different.

After experiencing the tragedy of father's life without love, there is another, more poignant, tragedy to consider: your own loveless life. Father's funeral scene is followed by one of your own. Project yourself twenty years into a future in which you have freely chosen not to rid yourself of the negative love patterns that have kept you from loving yourself and others, particularly *your* children. As the scene mentally unfolds, you can see your bitter, angry children standing above your casket as it is lowered into the ground. Your living spirit is witness as your children curse you for passing on to them the dreadful negative love disease that has blighted their lives. "Thank God, he's finally gone," they say. "We won't have to put up with *his* crap anymore. I wonder how much money was left us."

Does it make you angry or hurt to think that your children will damn you when you are dead? Seeing and hearing, psychically, the faces and voices of those who have suffered because of your negative love attachments to mother and father reaffirms dedication and total commitment to the task of learning to love yourself, your parents, and others. As our clients grieve over their own wasted lives there comes a moment when they stop and say, "Hey, wait a minute. *That's* not going to happen to *me*. I'm doing something about this Goddamn negative love crap so that my children, present or future, will *not* stand over my grave saying, 'Go to hell.' They will instead shed tears over the loss of my loving companionship, but that's all. I *will be* loved and cared for, and *I will* be loving and caring."

At the end of *A Christmas Carol* Scrooge saw his own neglected grave in the future, with his name engraved on the headstone. With this glimpse of the "future," our clients like Scrooge may well lament, "Oh, tell me I may sponge away the writing on this stone!" Dickens, too, understood the deep anguish of experiencing one's death in the future and the genuine rededication to a loving life that can arise from this vision.

For Nancy, Chris, and Laura, the worst was over. With great determination, they resolved that they would be the link to break the chain of negative love in their family.

CHAPTER X

THE ARMISTICE

Did you make any resolutions last New Year's Eve? Did you tell yourself that this year would be different; that this would be the year you solve *that* annoying problem or drop *that* distasteful habit? What happened? Did you stick to your decision and improve your life? If so, congratulations! Deciding to break a destructive habit and succeeding are genuine achievements.

Most people did not fare as well. They made their resolutions and embarked on a myriad ambitious self-improvement programs only to see their campaigns collapse and fail. It started out well enough, with some early improvement and a bright outlook, yet the old negative-love habits held on, only resulting in more self-condemnation, discouragement and frustration. Whether that bad habit is overwork, overeating, smoking, drinking, procrastination, or the most common problem of all, the inability to love, most people remain stuck in the trap of negative love.

Have you ever wondered why you go around and around and end up nowhere? The answer is not to be found in lack of will power or discipline. The importance of discipline and self-control in achieving our positive goals is vastly exaggerated! If that alone could do it, we would all be living positive, loving lives.

For most of us, most of the time, the adult intellect and the negative emotional child are locked in bitter, self-defeating conflict. And the bad-feeling kid is winning!

Difficult as it may be to admit, the truth is that your intellect is not running your life. Despite your best intellectual efforts and all you have learned about "right living" or the "good life" (however you may define them), your life is controlled by that rebellious, unloved child you were before you reached puberty. The more you struggle to control the child with discipline, the more frustrated you become. The negative love syndrome always wins out and it is the emotional child who controls our adult intellect. The intellect is a mere speck on the ocean of emotion, for it cannot control the child within. Each time the adult intellect attempts to make a change, the emotional child opposes; the little stubborn child within throws up obstacles, resistances, psychosomatic illnesses, excuses, lapses in memory, anything it can to defeat the best intentions for change. For sure we did not leave that child behind when we grew up. Most of us are not the civilized adults endowed with the ability to make rational choices that we pretend to be. Instead, we are mostly overgrown emotional children, *pretending* to be thinking adults. Behind the intellectual facade rages the fury of the emotions we felt as children.

The consequences of this battle within the self are widespread and devastating. Psychiatrists' offices, therapy groups, meditation classes, the entire spiritual growth and human potential movement, are filled largely with people searching for an end to the pain of the conflict between what they *know* and what they *feel*. The inner turmoil, confusion, pain, and distress caused by this conflict rob our lives of joy and promise. We neither think or feel to our full potential. When this intellect and child do battle, both are losers.

Although the worst of the emotion-intellect conflict occurs in adulthood, it begins before puberty, since the pre-pubertal child has a modicum of intellectual understanding in spite of the programming he receives daily from mother and father. He has some knowledge of right and wrong, and he knows what creates harmony and disharmony. Even as he is employing the devious maneuvers his parents are teaching him through negative love patterns, the child knows there is something better than the way he is living. As he grows up, his intellect learns about the loving potential in human relationships, even if he never saw it at home. "Other families were not the way mine was," he may discover with pained surprise.

"There really *is* something better than the life I knew as a child." However, when he tries to outdo mother and father, he experiences with full force the impact of the split between his intellect and his emotions. What he thinks he wants always eludes him, while what he gets is not what he thinks he wants. In truth, while the adult intellect watches helplessly, he gets exactly what his negative emotional child wants—negative love!

Unfortunately, the adult intellect remains the struggling victim of the emotional child even when it understands the damage brought on by the conflict. When one becomes a physiological adult, the intellect continues to grow and mature in knowledge and wisdom, while the emotions remain stuck in childhood. As the years pass, the gulf between them widens and deepens, creating an almost constant state of tension, anxiety, and confusion. After puberty, within severe limitations, the intellect can use its free will to act negatively or positively, depending on its sense of responsibility, desire, and training. Usually it unknowingly and ignorantly chooses to live out the negative programming under the control of the childhood emotions. The rationalization is, "That's the way I am. I can't help myself." Such a statement is one of the lies we live because of our negative love programs. We are *not* the conflicts and negativities we *adopted* from our parents. And yes, the power of the negative emotional child is such that it does not permit the intellect to cut the puppet strings of negative love to mother and father.

It is important to dispel the myth that you should "Be a parent to your child." Belief in this will be an albatross around your neck for life. The child is only a metaphor for the negatively arrested part of your emotions. The goal of the Quadrinity Process is for the child to *grow up* and no longer need parenting. You *can* get a loving divorce from mother and father, and in order to do so you must recognize that the emotional child within does not have to, and definitely should not, remain a child messing you up for life. Nor is it true that you are stuck with the cards your parents dealt you in your childhood. You can always *choose* to do something about it. Better to spend your energy helping that childish part of yourself grow up than to carry it around like a pet affliction.

Getting clear of mother and father, therefore, is not enough to end the debilitating conflict between the intellect and emotions. Mild feelings of depression and incompleteness tend to persist at this stage of the Process. The next step is for the adult intellect to take on and defy the emotional child and force it to stop causing trouble with its negative antics. Knowledge is power. The intellect has gained this power to defy the child with its newly acquired understanding of its problems.

Until the adult intellect learns that the real source of its problems is the negative emotional child, it is powerless to change. It can struggle valiantly and achieve small, hard-won gains, but it can never achieve lasting victory until it identifies and engages the real enemy. When the intellect does understand the true cause of its problems—negative love patterns— it can proceed to take responsibility for redirecting its life by opposing the force of the programmed child. "I am going to fight my resistant child who is wrecking havoc in my life," it decides.

This decision, when joined with determination and commitment, is not simply a New Year's resolution, soon to be broken. It understandably must create more tension, for it presages a new confrontation: the adult intellect versus the emotional child. The anticipation of any battle is a period of tense preparation. The insecure emotional child fears giving up its power. "What will be if I do?" The habit forces that drive it are powerful, and it resists the unknown future. For its part the intellect is righteously indignant at the emotional child for all the grief and misery it has caused. This combination of fear and anger is part of the natural uneasiness before the battle. There must be nothing tentative or hesitant in this new foray. The intellect must adhere to its decision to prevent the child from continuing to behave in its negative patterns.

The next step, then, in learning to love oneself is for the adult intellect to take on its negative emotional child in a bitch session. Here the intellect attacks the child's destructive, resistant behavior and demands that the child stop playing the negative tapes from childhood that are delaying their mutual progress toward fulfillment. Most of all the child must stop blocking the way of the adult intellect's efforts to make a better life for them, for in reality they are stuck with each other. The re-educated intellect, knowing what is best and what it needs, is angry with the negative child for preventing attainment of these positive goals.

The adult intellect begins to assume control over the negative emotional child through a mind revelation in the sanctuary. The intellect takes the child firmly and decisively in hand and says, "Look here, youngster! It's *you* who are to blame in this, not mother and father. *You're* doing this to me, and you're going to cut it out. Your nonsense has ruined my life long enough. Your negative garbage has caused all my problems. You've carried a grudge against everyone. You constantly fight me. You won't let go. You are *still* fighting with me. I don't need that negative love crap in my life any longer. From now on you're going to do what *I* say so that we can learn to be loving and happy."

To illustrate the dramatic resolution of the child-intellect conflict, I have drawn from the Process work of Chris. Like many clever, well-informed people, Chris experienced tremendous discomfort because of the contending parts of himself. Beneath his intellectual understanding of his own and other's problems, he now acknowledged that he had a severely arrested emotional child who effectively manipulated him and destroyed sought-for solutions to his love and work problems.

After a preparatory mind revelation, Chris's adult intellectual self was able to consummate his bitch session with his negative emotional child. (By this time he was no longer a Zombie on the Rocky Arc of Emotion.) Here are portions of his notes.

CHRIS: INTELLECT—CHILD BITCH SESSION

You're a child, but you're a bad one. You are misbehaving, and I am going to tell you what you've been fucking off about. I am supposed to be your intellect, and I'm a hell of a lot smarter than you are, and I know where it's at, and I'm telling you to shape up. You have been fucking us over, been mechanical, playing your Goddamn roles. Whenever it gets a little tough for you, you stupid twerp, you clam up. You cannot say what's on your mind. You won't express your feelings openly. Then what do you do? You can't even make a Goddamn decision. You fuck us over. Suspicious and distrustful, that's what you are. If somebody doesn't quite accept you totally, you see it as total rejection and play "poor baby". But no more! I've had enough of you. Too damn much!

You everlasting doubter! You refuse to believe in anything or anybody. Every time you face somebody who has a little authority or power, you back off, clam up. You can't make a decision. You paralyze us.

It's our life, you dumb little weepy twerp. Well, you're not going to be afraid of your shadow anymore. No more doubting, no more indecision. You're going to listen and understand how we've been hurting because of you.

You think you've got self-love? Bullshit! What you have is fear. You're a frustrated chickenshit. And when you can't have your own way, and you get a little scared, what do you do? You give me allergies, headaches, colds, you dumb, self-defeating little brat! Yes, you even make me impotent. And you think your fine appearance and a Goddamn cardboard fake image is what's going to protect us, but it doesn't. It just fucks us up and gets us hurt. I'm going to pound some sense into your head, you spoiled negative brat.

Now you're going to listen to me. No more crap. Stop your games. You stamp on others and then turn around and play "overresponsible." You think you have to take on the whole Goddamn world. Let's have a little response to me. We're going to confront each other and grow up. No more running away. Grow up, you damn, self-defeating, suffering bastard! You don't avoid conflict by running away.

I'm going to make you listen to me. No more sabotaging my growth, you little bastard, do you hear? Love to argue, do you? Think you're right and other people are wrong? Well, I know where that comes from, and you know where that comes from, and you're not going to keep it. I won't buy it anymore. You can't dominate me anymore.

(Crying) You bastard, you dumb, negative, self-

defeating shit! Resent me if you like, but you're not stopping me and you're not turning me off. No! No! I won't let you. I will not tolerate your sabotaging me anymore . . . You're always right, and you're always afraid, and you start and never finish and your wishy-washy vacillating never lets you make a decision yourself.

Child, you're bad! You really are powerfully bad . . . and I don't want to go through life like this, not living, always dominating and selfish. You're the spoiled-rotten, negative image of all the rotten negative traits of your father and mother.

Bob, during the process I focused on my child's negativity, not him. I feel so clean, not empty but clean inside and light. I feel so much cleaner than I did before—more, even, than after dealing with Mom and Dad. I don't feel anger, which was a defeated or frustrated quality to me. I'm feeling he won't really try so much anymore, and if the little bastard does, I'll take care of him.

Chris's intellect thus cleared himself with his child. In this session he unloaded the residual anger he had been carrying around since his defense of father. Chris prematurely thought that he had gained stewardship of his life. He felt as if he had finally whipped the ogres that had plagued him for so long. However the victorious feeling of conquest was short-lived. He was stunned out of his self-satisfaction when he learned that he, the adult intellect, the least suspected character in this life mystery was actually the most guilty.

Yes, the true villain is the intellect, who had just basked in the glow of victory over the child. It is far more guilty and stupid than the child because it shifted responsibility and blame everywhere except where it belonged, on itself. It blamed mother, father, the child, society, anyone it could in order to avoid seeing its own negligence and culpability. The intellect failed to take responsibility for its life, allowing the negative emotional child to act up and create the prob lems it then struggled in vain to solve. The intellect also made no effort to experience or understand the child and its needs. He failed to give the child understanding with no condemnation and compassion. Instead, the intellect made life hell for the child without mercy or restraint.

As we did with mother and father, we must abruptly look at the other side of the child-intellect coin. In a mind revelation the intellect is restrained by the spiritual self giving the child freedom to defend itself fearlessly against the earlier charges of the intellect. The child then berates the intellect and lets him have it.

"Yes, I'm guilty for programming you, big smartie intellect. Yah, I adopted all those negative traits from mother and father, *but you permitted it.* I was unaware and didn't know any better. You learned right from wrong. You were supposed to know better. You were smarter and bigger, and with your awareness your job was to help me and control me. I am just a little child. No wonder I don't wanna grow up. I'm staying split from you because you're no friend to me. You never really cared for me. You never loved me. You just used me as a scapegoat to avoid taking responsibility for yourself. The hell with you! If you won't care for me, *who will?* You big bully, you!"

The crucial importance of this procedure is that unless each part of the self accepts and understands the other parts, the total self remains divided and schizoid. The child, rejected by mother and father, has also been rejected by the intellect. All his life he has felt like an unwelcome guest in his own house. Now it is his opportunity to air his lifelong resentment at the treatment he received at the hands of his intellectual self.

Thus primed, Chris's child was ready to defend itself and put the responsibility and blame where they now rightfully belonged. Here is an excerpt of how Chris's child turned the coin and bitched at his intellect.

CHRIS: CHILD-INTELLECT BITCH SESSION

OK, Mr. Big Man, Big Shot Intellect. You S.O.B., now it's my turn. You yelled at me. You told me it was all my fault that we were getting screwed up and that I did this to you. Sure I did it to you. I fucked you over good to get back at you. Christ, I'm just a little kid. I counted on you to tell me what to do and make sure I did it, so I wouldn't get into trouble and feel so Goddamned guilty.

*And you, you just left me alone. Well, it's your
fault, too.*

*Jesus Christ! I haven't the words to argue with
you. If I had the words to argue with you I'd be
you; you're my other half. I need you, you bastard,
and you sit back and judge me and tell me to be
something I'm not. Well, I am what I am. If you
want me to shape up, then you help me by understanding me, not by being critical.*

*You talk about how I hurt you. You have only
a little feeling. I hurt 20,000 times more than you.
I* **need** *your help. I need you and you need me,
damn it! I'm smart enough to know that. Without
me you're a big hunk of dumb cement. Without
you, I'm just a big hunk of feeling, and I don't
know what to do or where to go. When you dump
on me, I'm going to dump back on you twenty
times as much. I can't help it, and you can, you
bastard. You must help both of us. Let me know
it's all right, and that you'll take care of us . . .*
I can't do it alone! Damn you!

Following these two bitch sessions, the intellect at the
child and the child at the intellect, it is possible to resolve
the problem of who is responsible for this unloveability.
Both must recognize that each was guilty but blameless, for
neither one knew any better due to the negative love programming. Having heard the enormous pain behind the plaints
and grievances of the child, the intellect becomes humbled
and contrite. It recognizes the truth of the child's protesta-
tions. It's time for a truce. The intellect walks up to the child,
puts an arm gently around it, and says something like this:

"Hey, little one, I never saw it from your point of view
before. You're right. I know now you weren't guilty. And I
know I wasn't guilty, either. I'm sorry for rejecting you.
Let's stop fighting and get together Really no one is to
blame. What do you say? Let's have a truce!"

The emotional child by now also recognizes that it has
been at war with its intellect all its life. It, too, is tired of
fighting and wants peace. Yet at first it approaches the idea
warily, since it has suffered greatly from the condemnation
and lack of understanding from everyone, especially the adult

intellect. The child tends to reply cautiously, saying, "I'll try if you will. You better damn well mean that you care, that you won't run away again. You're going to have to prove yourself!"

After the truce the emotional child begins to accept both the friendly motives of the intellect and the possibility of leaving childishness behind and growing up. With its modicum of intellectual ability the child recognizes there is no longer any reason to remain a child. It has prosecuted and defended mother and father, it has ended its conflict with the intellect and now has no legitimate cause for its dis-ease. The child fully understands that it no longer has to live according to the old *adopted* negative love games. Having experienced this crisis, it is free to choose the positive alternative.

The intellect has also reached a crisis point. At long last it takes responsibility for its past failure to exert control over the child and give it support.

Thus, the intellect and emotions finally learn that each is not the natural enemy of the other. They and mother and dad were guilty but not to blame. The spiritual self, overjoyed with the work, gives love, light, and nourishment to its child and intellect.

The war is over.

Hallelujah!

CHAPTER XI

THE JOY OF PLAY

The state of truce is not yet love. Although the hostilities have ended, and the groundwork for further growth and friendship between the adult intellect and the emotional child has been laid, more is needed. To consolidate the hopeful but cautious peace, the two lifelong adversaries need to learn to *play* together.

What does *play* mean to you? What part of your life do you consider to be play? Is your play truly lighthearted, joyous, and carefree? Can you play, both alone and with other people, in a way that renews, relaxes, and makes you feel good about being alive?

Most people cannot play in this positive manner. Instead, they do playlike things for serious, unplayful reasons. For example, if you play golf to beat your opponents, or to make business contacts, or perhaps to escape your unloving family, you are engaging in negative play. Unlike positive play, it doesn't leave you renewed for negative play only creates more anxiety and tension.

Those who say, "It's no fun unless I win," miss the point completely. Competition destroys the spirit of play. When it is *really play,* the score does not matter. Much of socializing at bars and getting high on alcohol is also not play, since its goal is the assuaging of loneliness and the hope of finding a bed partner to momentarily fill the empty cup of love. The need for attention or approval in play, as in work, always

stems from the negative love syndrome. Those who feel unloved and unlovable take that burden into all areas of living.

Some people consider their work play. This is a phony
rationale. Work is like play, either positive or negative, but it
always has a goal. Positive play is its *own* goal. Building a
swimming pool is work. Splashing in the water is play. Work
and true play are both needed for a harmonious life.

In positive play the spontaneous, childlike (not childish)
aspect of self is free to enjoy its inner flow. Whether tearing
around a tennis court or quietly listening to favorite music,
true play brings the joy of sheer living.

Sadly, many children never play with pleasure. Either they
are alone, feeling unloved and rejected, or they experience
play negatively by fighting, throwing things and disrupting
the good times of others. Negative play is another form of
negative love conditioning from unloving parents.

As an adult, playing is as important as anything you can do
with and for yourself. If you never experienced positive play
as a child, you will find it impossible to enjoy the richness of
adult play. Without play you will not only miss much of the
fun in life, but you will also not experience your own happy
self as a natural part of you. You may argue that childlike
playfulness is not important, that the "serious" you is the
real you. The truth is exactly the opposite. The real you is
joyous and spontaneous while the somber you is something
you adopted and learned to live with out of negative love to
your parents. If you rarely laugh with genuine delight, never
tell a joke, and in general feel little joy in life, it is certain
you have never learned to accept these fine human qualities
inherently as your own.

The saving grace is that despite your negative play experiences in childhood and the unplayful habits you may have
developed in adulthood, you *can* learn to play happily and
freely. You can be reunited with the suppressed childlike
part of yourself. Just as the emotional child can learn to end
its negative behavior, so the adult intellect can learn to accept
and enjoy the child's positive, childlike spontaneity. To be
whole again, the adult must simultaneously become less
childish and more childlike. To be of value, play must be a
direct experience. Only by experiencing the long-obscured
joyous self does the adult intellect accept and acknowledge
that which is most valuable in itself: the carefree, playful,

lovable, childlike personality.

All this is experienced on the evening of the play session, a happy highlight of the Process. The preceding eleven weeks have consisted of hard work and truly soul-searching experiences designed to purge negativity. On this evening the classroom is transformed into a festive play room, gaily decorated as if for a birthday party. Elaborate preparations assure an evening of special happy memories. The entire three-hour session is a party, with each client—child and intellect—the special guests.

The party begins with a mind revelation in which the group leader has the adult intellect take the emotional child on its lap and ask the child to teach it to play. The child agrees and is elated with its new, positive responsibility to teach its adult intellect the joys of play. The session then becomes a combined birthday and Christmas party, with all that the heart of a child desires: games and toys and good things to eat, lovingly prepared and shared. They romp and laugh together, tell stories, and dance. The entire group enters joyfully into the spirit of the evening. Those who have difficulty in playing catch the contagion of the fun and soon join in.

As the play session draws to a close, the adult intellect again takes its emotional child on its lap and thanks it for teaching it how to play. It tells the child how lovely it will be for both of them when it grows up and brings its happy, childlike positivity into the adult Trinity. The adult intellect knows now that joy and seriousness, laughter and responsibility, fun and commitment, can all be part of life in the present. For its part, the emotional child now truly realizes that it will not be harmed or further criticized and condemned by its intellect. It understands that it is only being asked to *drop* its childishness, while retaining its positive, childlike qualities. The emotional child now knows it loses nothing except its pain when it grows up.

If misery loves company, then joy loves company even more. The play session gives clients an opportunity to share positive experiences with their classmates in a social setting. After playing together, they learn a truth: that others want to reach out to them and share joy with them *if* they will allow it to happen. To enjoy oneself alone is not enough, for if it is to be full, life must be shared. The play session is the turning point of the journey toward reintegration of the

Quadrinity. Through direct experience both the emotional child and the adult intellect learn that the negativity of a lifetime was completely adopted from without—the true self within is both positive and joyful. Once this truth is fully comprehended, change for the better is inevitable.

In contrast to earlier sections of this book, the play session notes are filled with the lightheartedness of a happy child. Nancy had played as a child and was sometimes able to play as an adult. Secretly, however, she condemned herself for it. She considered play to be childish and irresponsible because of her negative emotional programming. As a result of her play session experiences, however, she learned the life-enhancing value of positive play:

> *It was like a beautiful fantasy, but it was far more than that. It was a reality that I helped create, because it was me as I am now and me as I am becoming. I felt close to all the people there and connected to the children in them and the child in me who now sees life with wonder and fearlessness. This was the child I knew was there. This was the exuberant, wonder-full child that had been denied. I'm so glad she's still around. My wish is to have this part of me stay in close touch with my adult intellect, each trusting, each willing to share the strengths they have with each other.*

At this point the relationship with mother and father is re-evaluated from a new perspective. Were they really all that bad? In preparation for learning to love mother and father, it is necessary to uncover and relive the moments from the past when they were affectionate, protective, and caring (or tried to be). Even the most negatively programmed person can find some positive scenes from childhood. Writing the Positive Emotional Autobiography with Mother and Father serves to balance out the negativity of the prosecution and defense sessions. Unlike the earlier negative emotional autobiographies, no goading with rude questions is necessary. Having gone this far, our clients have no difficulty recalling the beautiful and positive moments from the past. Now, after prosecuting and defending her parents and learning compassion for them, and for herself, Nancy is ready to see her parents and learning compassion for them, and for herself, Nancy is ready to see her parents in a different light. Here she recalls some of the happier times of her childhood:

NANCY: POSITIVE EMOTIONAL AUTOBIOGRAPHY

My mother is sewing a dress. The material is fine and white, and she is taking such care to make all the stitches tiny and even. My father is sitting just out of the ring of light at the table. He wonders at Mother's pleasure at having another baby when the other two have been so painful and worrisome. He feels proud of her and hopes everything will go well with this baby. This baby is me, and the dress is for me.

(At age two): We all take a ride to see Grandma's family. Mother and Grandma take turns holding me in the car. It is breezy, and I squeal. Daddy likes taking everybody in the car and Mother wants her aunts to see me. That's nice. I know she thinks they will like me. I love bouncing around in the car and feeling the trees zoom by. When we go by a post, it sounds as though we cut if off, just with the sound . . . Zap. It's nice to go bouncing along all together.

After washing up for supper, my father puts Honey and Almond Cream on his hands. There is too much, so he takes my hands between his and gives me some of the warm, smooth cream to use on my hands. Then we go together to the table, both smelling the same, both ready to eat supper. It's a nice feeling.

In the kitchen, wrapped in a big towel after my bath, I feel warm and safe. My mother has my nightgown hanging over the heater in the other room, and when I get dry, I will have a warm, dry nightie to put on. My father made popcorn for us. My brother is practicing the piano, and it makes happy tinkling sounds.

My sixth birthday. My mother makes me a pretty dress, red with white polka dots, and she laughs when I ask her how she made it without my finding out. She shows me where she has kept it while she was working on it. My father takes us all to the zoo in our new car. We stop for gas in the city, and when my father says it is my birthday, the man gives us each a sucker. I am pleased and proud.

On Halloween, when I am six, my mother and father get us ready to go out. Mother helps with the costumes, while father shows me how to make a noisemaker out of a spool with notched edges and string to pull it. When the string is pulled, the spool edges make a loud noise. Then he burns a cork and blackens our faces with it. We are given a flashlight to carry.

Later on, mother keeps us feeling like a family. We go on lots of Sunday picnics, some of them at a beach. I can still smell the special wet smell that goes along with swimming as a child: mother and the other grown-ups sitting in the shade, my brother bringing buckets of water from the lake so I can make sand castles. I remember the lovely, gritty egg salad sandwiches and the ride home in the open car, everything filled with sand, my toes scratching in my sandals, everyone relaxed, sometimes singing things like, "Row, row, row your boat!"

There is something special about thunderstorms in the summer. We all sit together after running around to close the windows. My mother counts the seconds between the flash of lightning and the sound of thunder, and we try to figure out how far away it had been. I love it, feeling excited and safe.

My mother loves to listen to me telling her about the books I read. She seems really interested in them, not like she is judging whether or not they were "good" or "instructive" but in what seems to me to be a rather childlike manner. This is a new idea to me. It is a sharing with her that I am unaware of at the time. Her interest is not as an adult thinking, "What a bright daughter," but as another human being on pretty much the same level.

> She *was the one who encouraged and supported*
> *me because she was* there *with me. I realized that a*
> *lot of positive relationships were there with my*
> *mother that I have not been aware of. I have ig-*
> *nored my mother's warm human role in this, not*
> *being perfect, just interested. They were both*
> *really doing their best.*

The importance of these recollections is the opportunity they afford to *reconsider the past* unclouded with negative love patterns. For the first time in adulthood Nancy saw her childhood years with genuine appreciation for the goodness those years held. She can describe her early years without intellectualizing or covering over any unacceptable feelings of anger, fear, or resentment. She knows exactly what happened and how she feels about it. She is free of negative feelings about her childhood and will carry the positive feelings with her for the remainder of her life.

After writing her positive emotional autobiography, Nancy found herself feeling more positive than ever before. Her depressed moods began to lift, her body posture straightened, and her facial expressions took on a new brightness.

To further solidify the newly positive attitude toward mother and father, clients are asked to describe how their parents' virtues have affected their lives positively. Here is how one young man described his insights.

> *My parents were both active, athletic people,*
> *and from them I learned to enjoy my body and*
> *keep myself in good physical condition. My father*
> *was strong, quick, and well-coordinated, and he*
> *taught me to love physical exercise. I love playing*
> *tennis and baseball, as well as any good physical*
> *workout, thanks to the example he set.*
>
> *Both Mom and Dad loved beauty of all kinds.*
> *They appreciated subtlety and detail, qualities I*
> *have adopted in my photography. My father was*
> *original and inventive in solving problems. Many*
> *times in my life I have felt great satisfaction in*
> *solving problems or creating new designs that have*
> *flair, simplicity, and beauty, the qualities he loved*
> *most.*

Best of all, my parents loved to laugh and smile.
Like them, I love telling good stories and laugh
easily. People like my hearty laugh and ready smile.
The laugh is my father's, the smile is my mother's.
God bless them both for the beauty they passed
along to me.

The play session and the positive emotional autobiography provide a solid foundation for the integration of the Quadrinity in the Closure session.

CHAPTER XII

CLOSURE:
THE DAY OF RE-BIRTH

The negative love syndrome survives on the vain hope that if we are like our parents someday they will finally love us. All who are neurotics hope that somehow they will finally gain a resounding "Yes!" to their unspoken childhood plea, "I'm just like you, Mommy and Daddy. *Now* will you love me?"

These hopes are sad and pitiful. Negative behavior does not lead to positive love. No matter how much like your parents you become, or how tirelessly your struggle to rebel and rise above their negative example, mother and father will never love you the way your emotional child needs and wants: selflessly, wholeheartedly, and with nothing asked in return. One empty cup cannot fill another. Until you experience this truth, you live helplessly imprisoned in darkness. You can become a growth experience addict and search for love needlessly outside yourself, but as long as you continue looking for mother's and father's love from the past, you are stuck.

It's been on a long journey of discovery. You have learned that mother and father are the source of your love problems, yet are blameless victims themselves. You know you have been at war with yourself, and that you too were blameless. You have learned that to be fully alive is to be able to play joyfully. All of this has been preparation for the ultimate truth: You are loveable. You are love. You are part of the "Light" (the universal Godhead who is love) and as such you are in *the Light.* Underneath the layers of negativity is your real perfect positive essence. Your spiritual self. Positivity does not have to be learned. It must simply be uncovered.

When the lie of negative love has been exposed, it must fall away and die for lack of nourishment. Once the inner void is filled with innate self-love, the motivating force behind the negative patterns disappears. Why vainly seek pseudo-love from the past when you can give true love to yourself in the present?

Of course, there is nothing new in saying that the answer lies within. Psychiatry, the human potential movement, and various religious disciplines all give voice to this wisdom. How frustrating it is, then, to search in vain within for life's most highly prized experience. If love is inside us, why can't we find it?

Not until the puppet strings from mother and father are cut and love is uncovered on the emotional, intellectual, and spiritual levels of being can you discover your own source of love—you.

Dr. Julius Brandstatter, an old friend and Process teacher, has aptly expressed it this way: "Negative love is passed from generation to generation in almost all people and families. Is it any wonder that we have a sick and getting-sicker society? The corrections begin with oneself. And the most evil of all evils is negative love. It is a sickness in itself, alarmingly contagious, reaching epidemic proportions with no immunity for anyone. Until this is understood, there is little chance to arrest this virulent disease which threatens to engulf everyone in time."

Negative love is replaced with true love in a culminating event—the Closure section. Although the negative love traits have been let go, the positive emotional child is still separate from the other parts of himself. The child within must now be taught literally to grow up and take his place as a loving, integrated aspect of its adult mind Trinity. The victory of the preceding twelve weeks has been preparation for this climactic moment.

This magnificent event is marked by a ceremony befitting its significance. It is a celebration of love and renewal. The light colorful apparel of the graduates blends with the lovely floral setting of the classroom. The weary weeks of pain give way to the joy of self-discovery and love.

The Closure mind revelation lasts two and a half hours, yet to all seems like minutes. It is a solemn affirmation of loving commitment to oneself. It is a confirmation of the Light we are. One phase of life is ending; another is beginning. The ritual serves to seal the agreement with oneself to leave the negative realm of the past and willingly emerge into the new life of positive self-acceptance and love.

Learning to love is accomplished by teaching the adult intellect and the emotional child three final steps. They are (1) acceptance; (2) forgiveness (in which "Turn the other cheek" is no longer an admonition but an internal state of being); (3) uncompromising *love*. The child finally receives the love it needs from the most important being in its existence, *not* mother or father, but its *own* adult self. Here lies the essence of the self-love experience. With no negative blocks to prevent it, love flows freely between the two selves, adult intellect and emotional child.

In the final session, the actual love exchange begins with a mind revelation taking the child back year by year to infancy. The intellect with total empathy and compassion reaches out for its child, takes it into its arms, feels the warmth of the baby's body, and tastes the salt of its tears. Knowing the child is no longer to be blamed, for it did not know what it had done, the adult intellect expresses its heartfelt understanding with no condemnation. It experiences understanding with no condemnation, compassion, acceptance, honest forgiveness, and true love for its child. The child's cup of love is filled from the most important being in its world, its own adult intellectual self. The emotional child's quest for self-love is finally realized.

The child is now willing to grow up. The intellect and spiritual self lovingly support and watch the child gradually grow, year by year. Tears of joy and relief flow freely as the child *feels,* for the first time, the warmth of complete loving acceptance. Beginning with this moment, the child within *knows* love as a total experience.

Finally, the emotional self arrives at the same chronological age as the adult intellect. There is now a positive emotional adult in place of the negative emotional child. As they lovingly face each other in their sanctuary, they again share the five steps of love: understanding with no condemnation, compassion, acceptance, forgiveness, and love. In the most beautiful experience of the Process the now positive emotional self, newly re-educated adult intellect, and perfect spiritual self are wedded in the "Light." The summit has been reached. It's a spiritual experience of enlightment. The search for self is over. The goal of love is achieved.

With this new, solid, centered state of well-being, the Trinity is ready to make lasting peace and create a new positive loving rapport with mother and father. (The experience is valid whether mother and father are living or dead.) The newly re-educated and loving Trinity now completely understands and accepts that mother and father were not the cause of negative love patterns, merely the innocent transmitters. Therefore, the Mind Trinity stops blaming the parents who were unwitting carriers of the disease.

Mother's spirit is brought into the sanctuary. The new loving Trinity walks up to her, looks warmly at her, embraces her, and says, "Mother, dear, I now understand you more than ever and, yes, I understand you better than you do yourself. I don't condemn you anymore. Mother, I have found real compassion for you. I warmly accept you and totally forgive you, for you did not know what you did to me, to Father, or to the children. With all my heart, I give you my true love."

Then father's spirit is brought into the sanctuary, and the same love exchange is repeated.

Giving love to mother and father is the final step in cutting the parental puppet strings, achieving emotional autonomy and a loving divorce. If your parents are dead, their nonphysical mind spirits can join yours and deeply experience the beauty of love realized. If they are still alive, the loving exchange is repeated in person as soon as possible following Closure.

Free at last of negative love, the newly integrated Trinity rejoins its physical body to become a living Quadrinity. The newly cleansed Mind Trinity can now reprogram the computerlike brain so that the total Quadrinity can live a positive loving normal life. With this achieved, Closure is complete.

Closure is an emotional catharsis, cleansing and purifying. It is the healing, the closure of the wounds opened during the Process experience.

By Closure most of the negative traits have been organically removed. Yet the death of negative love patterns does not bring an immediate end to all negative behavior. Habits of a lifetime sometimes die a hard death. The persistence of negative patterns after their cause has been removed is similar to the phantom limb phenomenon, in which an amputee continues to feel as if the severed arm or leg were still there. The gradual pace at which residual negative patterns disappear is similar to this neurological phenomenon.

Awareness and patience are needed. Like erasing a chalk mark on a blackboard, the first cleansing stroke will make the image fainter but not completely obliterate it. Usually the second or third swipe is sufficient to clean it completely.

Without *roots* the negative trait cannot survive the regular use of the recycling techniques that the clients are taught.

For recycling and awareness to be effective, however, one must *choose* to use them. One can either use the techniques to consolidate one's gains or remain the victim of the residual, now false negative habits. One man experienced his responsibility for his future in this way:

> *During the week I heard my perfectionistic doubter say (out of negative love to both my parents), "Bob's mind revelations are simply autosuggestion, they don't have any substance. I can make them fail if I want to. They are not perfect techniques." Later I understood how wrong I was. If I* want *them to fail, I* lose. *If I want them to* work, *I* win. *They can work if I want them to, for otherwise I could not have done the bitch sessions and every other aspect of the work, which had such a profound effect on me. So I want this final mind revelation to work so I can live a loving life. Then I recalled the orange and lemon mind revelation and how I salivated, and I realized that this wasn't just fantasy. Why did I salivate and my mouth pucker when I ate the imaginary lemon? Could I have come so far and still fail final processing? Yes, I could, but I won't. I'm going to win. It's true my problems have been with my mind, so I will* accept *the mind revelations to cleanse my mind and find love.*

Win he did. This man is an internationally acclaimed concert musician. Although his performances were flawless, prior to the Process his nervous anxiety caused his hands to perspire and his mouth to go dry. Today his stage fright has vanished; he performs with relaxed self-confidence. He was delighted when a recent newspaper review praised not only his musical genuis but also his new poise and stage presence.

When the new state of love is consolidated, life changes are dramatic. Problems of unlovability, fear, guilt, anxiety, despair, anger, and psychosomatic illnesses begin to vanish. Migraines, impotence, paranoia, and some forms of allergies disappear. Not surprisingly, experiencing true love also changes one's attitudes toward all relationships. Visiting with mother and father, no longer a dutiful ordeal, becomes a time of warmth and love. Parents are delighted to be on the receiving end of the love they so seldom experienced. Husbands and wives either draw closer together in love, or they separate lovingly. Those who love truly, relate lovingly and positively with their children. Having discovered how negative love patterns crippled them in childhood, parents are especially determined not to pass them on to their children. They also report with obvious delight the willingness of their children to respond to their new, loving parenthood.

One such response came from the grown daughter of a fifty-six-year-old woman: "Dear Bob, My mom has become a real mother to me, filling my life with much love and joy and comfort. She credits this development to you and therefore I thank you for all you've done for us. Sincerely, Betty Silverman, daughter of Janet Silverman." She appended the following postscript: "When the tree bears fruit, the gardener smiles and rejoices in the success of his efforts."

With love one also learns to accept people. When they are negative one is able to understand the truth behind their facade and therefore be more understanding while avoiding entanglement in their patterns of negativity.

We are often asked how is it possible to be so positive in a world so negative? Even if you love yourself, how can you live lovingly in an unloving world?

Refusing to live fully in the world until it is perfect is another aspect of the negative love program from your parents. When the mind Trinity is re-educated and free of the blinders put on it by the childhood program, one sees that the world is just not perfect, but simply the way it is. Each of us has power over only a small fragment of it. If the great spiritual teachers of the past, Moses, Buddha, Jesus, and Mohammed, could not eradicate the unloving evil in the world who are we to think we can? It is enough to eradicate the evil in oneself.

However, the world may not be as unloving as you think. Patterns of negative love close our eyes to much of the goodness, beauty, and love around us. All we see is what we know. If we knew only fear, anger, jealousy, and stupidity as a child, that may be all we have allowed ourselves to see as adults. Once we experience love on all four levels of being, we are able to experience love all around us.

Achieving self-love and love for others is a powerful, dramatic, and beautiful experience but it is not a "high." Peaks of elation are often followed by valleys of despair; this is not the Quadrinity Process way. True love replaces this cycle of highs and lows with a broad climbing plateau, and from this plateau you can evolve to still higher spaces.

This does not mean that you will never have moments of unhappiness, grief, righteous indignation, or pain. Living "in love" means flowing through the obstacles of life and experiencing them without feeling overwhelmed, inundated, and depressed.

The death of a close relative or friend, for example, may leave one grieving for the loss of companionship. With self-love, however, death no longer brings severe depression and remorse for past wrongs left uncorrected or deeds of kindness left undone. The expression of loving grief soon yields to loving acceptance. In the workaday world, too, when things go wrong, either through miscalculation or the dishonesty of others, your response of acceptance and determination to know better the next time will make it easier. Righteous indignation at those who treat you unfairly is valid and should be experienced. Being rejected by someone you may want to love may also bring temporary sadness, but with true love for yourself it will not lead to depression. With acceptance as the key word, you can recognize in all *honesty* that the problem lies with the rejector not you. It's then better that the affair is short-lived.

Those experiencing the journey through the patterns of negative love to the transformation of self-love often write to us. The following report, highly abbreviated, relates the experience of a trained behavioral scientist.

Immediately following Closure I felt drained. I then played my old invalidation trip and told myself, "This isn't as much different as I had expected." However I did feel something else going on inside of me, some further, undefined, internal process that had been started but certainly not finished.

Later I got depressed and angry, with a feeling that this whole damn painful Process had been just one more search for magic like a Goddamn little kid, and here I am let down again. This feeling came and went for a week or more. I even felt resentful at having a last assignment to write up the final session.

Gradually I became aware that I was organically changing. I continued to follow the post-Process homework prescriptions. Throughout the Process I had been more aware of playing invalidation games with myself and other putdowns. Now, after the Process, these habits are surprisingly losing their control over me. I tried to revert to my old ways of feeling and seek escape by telling myself that I was not really responsible for my life and that the world was too big and complex a machine for powerless me, but this didn't work. I was stuck with the knowledge that I was really in charge of my own life and living negative love patterns had no meaning any more.

Looking back now, some time after Closure, I can see changes in me—many that I feel inside and some that other people have told me they see. I spent much of my life being sick and exhausted in bed. Surprise! I have not been sick since Closure. No colds or flu.

I feel more confident in all areas of my life than ever before. The myraid little questions and paranoid fears that add up to "Suppose he or she gets mad at me," or "Am I OK?" just don't occur much, and when they do, they are obviously so silly that they fall apart when I look at them and use my post-Process tools.

All my life I have hidden and felt personally

attacked and threatened whenever someone disagreed with me. Now I find myself listening, and agreeing or disagreeing openly, without my habitual defensiveness or attack.

The frustrations and barriers which I met in the past still occur, but my depression over them does not. Most of my life people have told me, or shown me, that I appear cold, uncaring, aloof, and critical, at least until they got to know me. And with a front like that, not many people made the attempt. In the past months, people have commented on my approachability and caring and made comments like, "You've gotten so loose. It's great!"

Prior to the Process I avoided being with my mother out of anger and fear. I paid holiday "duty calls" and always with a heavy feeling of guilt, intolerance, and a desire to get out fast. She pushed my buttons so strongly I often couldn't get in her door without feeling zapped, and phone calls left me seething and swearing and taking it out on my family.

Ever since the Process I have felt comfortable with her and have expressed my love for her. I have actively taken care of her and felt warm and loving. She still says the same things and complains in the same way, with her subtle and not-so-subtle putdowns. I see them clearer than ever, but now the old instant rage/guilt/attack/run away feelings don't follow. She's just a human being with wants, needs, pains, feelings, and habits like anyone else.

Although my father died early in my life, I have at last made my peace with him. I am sorry he died before I could physically experience his warmth and have a chance to be a living, loving friend with him.

I am becoming a firmer and more lovingly supportive father to my three daughters. My wife has told me of the great changes she sees in me. She says I am much stronger, a trait she describes as a mixed blessing. She can count on me more, but it is harder to manipulate me. She also describes me as being much more sensitive to her moods and feelings. My old ways of denying myself, hiding, and not telling her how I felt about things are changing now, too. Our relationship, which was wooden, dependent, and unreal, is turning into a vital human exchange between two live people.

I now know and feel to my depths that no one is responsible for my life except me. What I do is up to me. The real barriers and limitations I meet are not out there but within. Like it or not, I am in charge of my attitudes and my life—and I like it. I have long periods of respect and love for myself I rarely experienced before. I wish everyone could experience the best of what I have experienced the past two years.

Lastly, I want to say that I continue to change and grow. My life is flowing, and I am on a journey, not knowing quite where my path goes but joyously content to follow my heart. Accepting my loving spiritual "Light" essence has made the acceptance of myself a true love experience.

Here is how Tom, a young law student, described a visit to his parents shortly after Closure:

As soon as I arrived home, I saw that on my parents' side nothing had changed. I saw all the old patterns, but instead of participating in the insanity, I felt understanding, no condemnation, compassion, total acceptance, forgiveness, and selfless love. I felt better every day I was home.

The first day I was home, Mom was rushing around trying to get things ready for Christmas. I told her I had something important to tell her, and she had to be still. She said, "Son, even the important things in life have to be sandwiched between ... "

"Well," I said, "I just want you to take a couple minutes, put things aside and listen. I want you to **hear** *me." Finally she stopped. The difficulty in getting her to stop for a minute only increased the feeling of compassion I had for her. We were sitting upstairs, and she had her arms folded across her*

belly. She was very tense and started crying a little.

"I wanted you to relax and hear me, Mom."

"I can't relax! I listen the way I want to!"

"Okay, that's fine, Mom. I understand. Mom, I just wanted you to know that I love you."

"Is that all?" she asked incredulously.

I took her in my arms. "Yes, Mom. You know that I will **always** *love you."*

"You don't have to say that. Always. That's implied." I understood her anxiety about "always."

"I do love you," I said. As I held her and gave her my selfless love, she let go a big flood of guilt.

"It was stupid to have you as a child when I was so young." She was crying as I held her, feeling the flow of love between us. I knew I **could** *give love and giving it felt wonderful.*

"I am forty-eight, and I'm still not grown up," she sobbed. "But you're twenty-six and you seem to be all there."

"Right on, Mom. I am all here, and I love you."

"You feel like you're all together, like somewhere along the line you picked up the ball, like you picked up the load."

"Right on, Mom!"

"You had me worried that you had some disease or something was terribly wrong. I'm glad you told me that you love me. I love you, too."

That night Dad was in bed reading the newspaper before he went to sleep. I was trying to think of how to make "I love you" explode into his heart and mind. I was wrapping some gifts, and I thought, "The time is perfect. I don't want to wait one more minute. I want to give this to him now." So I went into his room, and this is what happened:

"Dad, there's something important I want to tell you." He put down his newspaper. "Dad, I just want you to know that I love you," and I took him in my arms and kissed him. It felt very warm. Though there was no big explosion he was obviously moved. I felt understanding, no condemnation, compassion, total forgiveness, acceptance, and

selfless love for Dad during the whole visit. The "I love you" was just part of that continuum. Before I left, Mom said she couldn't understand it. I hadn't been so loving since before my brother was born when I was four.

Some months later I decided that I wasn't going to follow Dad's footsteps and become a lawyer, but intended to become a contractor instead. Mom and Dad became anxious and uptight. Instead of lashing out defensively or closing up, I just continued to give them both my selfless love. That love eased their disappointment and helped them to accept my decision. Our relationship has been beautiful ever since and it continues to grow.

When we reach this state of love for self, our parents, and others, we are able to make the positive long-term changes in our lives. Dreams become reality. Like Tom, we can move into more satisfying careers or we may discover that what we are doing is more rewarding than we thought. Our relationships become solid, or lovingly we move on to new ones.

This letter arrived at the Center just the other day:

Dear Bob,

It has been just a year since I finished the Process, and I am fulfilling your parting request to let you know what happened to me.

The news is unbelievably good. I have finally achieved the kind of loving relationship with a woman I always longed for. I'm no longer fearful and rejecting of women as I used to be. The hell of self-doubt and emptiness is gone. My tendencies to be suspicious and judgmental as an excuse to reject people have evaporated. I'm no longer on guard all the time. I can remember laughing, joking, and exuding enthusiasm as a cover-up for my old negative feelings when I was with people—and then going home and feeling so lonely and inadequate that I'd have fantasies of killing myself to end the pain. All this is done and gone. Thank God.

Bob, everything has changed for me. Now when

I have a good time with people, either at work or socially, it's for real. I keep feeling good after I've left them. I've grown sure of myself and open to other people. For the first time in my life I have both men and women as friends, and life is very good. Loving Sally happened in such an easy, flowing way it seemed the most natural thing in the world. We are friends, companions, lovers, and roommates, and we plan to be married soon. We are very happy and we want to give to each other because giving is now so real and so good. Just like you said, it's as simple as that.

She loves the country as much as I do. Just last month on our trip to Oregon we found the piece of land we've both been dreaming about, and it is going into escrow next week. We expect to be ready to move there for good in a couple of years.

We both send our love and deepest gratitude and our hope that you will be at our wedding. All my love,

Carl

Words pale next to experience. Reading brings knowledge, but experience brings *knowing*. When you experience the truth of self-love, you will find that *you* are the answer you have been waiting for. You no longer need to search for love or struggle to gain it from others. When you learn how to contact the "Light" source within yourself, you can drink from your own cup of love and share the joyous overflow. For you are love!

AFTERWORD

The Quadrinity Process is a unique, experiential, structured and artful integration of original concepts and techniques the result of which is fundamental change in attitudes and behaviors toward self and others. The Process has a lasting effect on individuals because it identifies and eliminates negative love patterns which are the root causes of all emotional problems. It transforms compulsive, negative, self-defeating behavior, moods, and attitudes into naturally positive, self-enhancing behavior, moods, and attitudes. As a result of the Process the individual becomes both free and autonomous.

The Quadrinity Process was created by Bob Hoffman in 1967. Initially the Process was structured in a 13-week format comprised of weekly group meetings three to five hours long, assignments to be done individually by the student, and one-to-one sessions between the student and assigned teacher. Using the fundamental principles and elements of the original Process, Bob Hoffman re-designed the Quadrinity Process to an 8-week format in 1984, and then in 1985 into the current 7-day intensive residential program. These changes have made the Process more dynamic, more effective, and more powerful. They have also made the Quadrinity Process more accessible to the people throughout the world in terms of logistics, time, and money.

Students have come from all over the USA, Canada, Europe, and Latin America. They include doctors, lawyers, entrepreneurs, business executives, public administrators, therapists, psychiatrists, psychoanalysts, psychologists, priests, nuns, rabbis, ministers, teachers, professors, writers, musicians, artists, dancers, homemakers, teenagers, and senior citizens. They include workaholics, perfectionists, overachievers, childhood victims of emotional, physical, sexual abuse, alcohol and drug addiction, people who were themselves alcoholics, drug users, child abusers, people who could not accept their own success, people who were unhappy with their lives and wanted to make a change.

Bob Hoffman created the concept "quadrinity" and designed the quadrinity symbol. The quadrinity is the four (quad) interactive aspects of one's self: physical body, emotional self, intellectual self, and spiritual or higher self. The quadrinity model is a framework for understanding human behavior. The four aspects of self are interactive and form a complex feedback system. The Process creates a harmonious integration of the four aspects of self and results in total self-acceptance, self-forgiveness, and self-love.

Since the Process was created by Bob Hoffman, it has been referred to as the Fischer-Hoffman Process, The Hoffman Process, The Hoffman Quadrinity Process, The Quadrinity Process, and The Quadrinity Intensive Process. The Hoffman Institute and its licensed affiliates are the only authorized teachers of the Process. The Process is powerful. It should be taught only by those who have been thoroughly trained and validated by the Institute.

It is my hope that the knowledge I have shared with you in this book will help make your journey through life more fulfilling.

For more information about the Process and teacher training, write or call:

Hoffman Institute USA
223 San Anselmo Avenue, Unit 4
San Anselmo, CA 94960
phone: (415) 485-5220
fax: (415) 485-5539

Hoffman Institute Centers

The Hoffman Institute and its licensed affiliates worldwide are the only authorized teachers of the Quadrinity Process. The Quadrinity Process was created and developed by Bob Hoffman as described in the Preface of this book. Process groups are scheduled regularly throughout the year in Europe, Australia, Canada, Latin America, and the United States.

USA: California
223 San Anselmo Ave., Unit 4
San Anselmo, CA 94960
phone: 1-415-485-5220
or: 1-800-506-5253
fax: 1-415-485-5539

USA: Virginia
5504 Ivor Street
Springfield, VA 22151
phone: 1-703-941-8577
  or: 800-598-7778
fax: 1-703-914-2733

USA: Wisconsin
1015 Oakland Ave.
Madison, WI 53711
phone: 1-608-250-6676

Argentina
Santa Fe 3796 2°F
(1425) Capital Federal, Argentina
phone/fax: 011-541-833-2872

Australia
Suite 3, 230 Toorak Road
South Yarra, Victoria 3141
Australia
phone: 011-61-39-826-2133
fax: 011-61-39-826-2144

Austria
Reisnerstrasse 35
A-1030 Vienna
Austria
phone: 011-431-713-9980
fax: 011-431-713-9981

Brazil: Sao Paulo
Av. Padre Pereira de Andrade, 100
Boçcava
Sao Paulo, SP, CEP 05469-000
Brazil
phone: 011-55-11-832-7892
Fax: 011-55-11-261-9570
or-fax: 011-55-11-831-2680

Brazil: Belo Horizonte
Rua Itapemirim, 433 - Serra
30.240/000 Belo Horizonte, MG
Brazil
phone: 011-55-31-227-8512
fax: 011-55-31-223-2786

Canada
15 Parkwood Drive
Cambridge, Ontario
N1S 3K6 Canada
phone: 1-519-622-4060
or: 1-800-741-3449
fax: 1-519-622-9684

England
66 Caistor Road
London SW11 8PZ
England
phone: 011-44-181-333-2222
fax: 011-44-181-333-9222

France
Jagerhausleweg 32
DW-79104 Freiburg
Germany
phone: 011-49-761-55-4585
fax: 011-49-761-56-843

Germany: Berlin
Postfach 304 004
D-10725 Berlin
Germany
phone: 011-49-30-217-6613
fax: 011-49-30-217-7719

Germany: Dusseldorf
Bredelaerstrasse 59
40474 Dusseldorf
Germany
phone: 011-49-211-452-365
fax: 011-49-211-470-7950

Hong Kong
4/FL Dina House Ruttonjee Center
11 Duddell Street
Central, Hong Kong
phone/fax: 011-852-2-688-5307

Italy
Via M.A. Colonna 42
20149 Milano
MI Italy
phone: 011-392-32-5673
fax: 011-392-32-72-217

Spain
San Francisco 1-3°
01001 Vitoria
Spain
phone/fax: 011-34-45-288-896

Switzerland
Seestrasse 15 A
8805 Richterswil
Switzerland
phone: 011-411-786-1484
fax: 011-411-786-1530

Please send me information on:

❑ The 7 1/2-Day Intensive Quadrinity Process
❑ Dates of future Quadrinity Processes in my area
❑ Quadrinity Process Introductory Evenings
❑ Quadrinity Process Teacher Training Program

NAME _____

ADDRESS_____

CITY _____STATE__ZIP_____

TELEPHONE (   ) _____

Hoffman Institute USA
223 San Anselmo Ave., Unit 4
San Anselmo, CA 94960
Phone: (510) 485-5220
Fax: (510) 485-5539